ARDOCH 2000

ARDOCH 2000

A brief history of Ardoch Parish
to the end of the Second Millennium

William C. Hutchison, B.Sc., Ph.D., M.I.Biol., F.R.S.C.

Ardoch 2000 Millennium Committee

Cover illustration:
Aerial view of Braco village in the 1980s by Ray Mitchell.

Frontispiece:
The village from the north in 1950.

© William C. Hutchison, B.Sc., Ph.D., M.I.Biol., F.R.S.C.

Published in the year 2000 by
Ardoch 2000 Millennium Committee
01786 880727

The author has asserted his moral rights.

No part of this book may be transmitted or reproduced in any form or by any means mechanical or electrical including photocopy, without permission in writing, except by a reviewer in connection with a newspaper, magazine or broadcast.

British Library Cataloguing-in-Publication Data.
A catalogue record for this book is available from the British Library.

ISBN 0 9537827 0 0

Printed by
Cordfall Limited
0141 572 0878

Contents

Illustrations	6
Preface	7
Introduction	9
Early History	11
The Dark Ages and the Medieval Period	14
The Seventeenth and Eighteenth Centuries	15
Roads and Bridges	18
The Development of the Village	21
The Churches	23
Schools	27
Hotels and Inns	35
The Village Halls	39
The Railway	41
The Principal Estates	43
John G. McKendrick – A Lad o' Pairts	52
The Suicides' Graves	54
The Toll Houses	55
Some Agricultural Matters	56
The War Memorial	59
Police, Medical and Veterinary Services	63
Shops and Trades	65
Local Government	70
Recreational and Social Activities	70
Index	77

Illustrations

Braco from the north, 1950	2
1866 Map of Ardoch parish	8
Braco from the air	9
The Roman Fort from the north-east	11
The ditches of the Roman Fort	13
Bridges over the Knaik	18
Cataracts on the Knaik	19
Church Street in 1898	20
Braco from the north in the 1890s	21
Ardoch Church, 1999	22
Ardoch Church in 1910	23
Greenloaning Manse in 1908	25
Church Tower in 1999	26
Children of Greenloaning, 1947	28
Children of Greenloaning School, 1999	28
Old School and Schoolhouse, Greenloaning	30
The new school at Greenloaning, 1999.	31
Braco Nursery School, 1999	32
Braco School, 1999	32
Braco Primary 1–4, 1999	33
Braco Primary 5–7, 1999	33
Feddal Road in 1910	34
Greenloaning Inn in the 1890s	35
Braco Hotel in the 1890s	36
'Ardochlea', 1999	36
Ardoch Hotel in 1918	36
Braco Hotel in Front Street around 1948	37
Braco Hotel, 1999	37
Allanbank Hotel in the 1890s	38
Allanbank Hotel, 1999	38
Greenloaning Inn being renovated, 1999	39
Greenloaning Station in the 1920s	40
Greenloaning Station in modern times	40
Allanbank Hotel in the early 1900s	41
Greenloaning Station, 1999	42
Ardoch House in 1898	43
South entrance to Ardoch House in 1899	44
South entrance of Ardoch House, 1999	44
Main entrance to Ardoch House	45
Braco Castle in 1922	46
Braco Castle, 1999	47
Old Feddal House in 1898	49
Feddal Castle in 1909	49
Orchil House in 1898	50
Orchil House, 1999	50
The Old House of Orchil, 1999	51
The Rottearns Toll House	55
Front Street in 1899	56
The War Memorial, 1999	58
The War Memorial in 1922	58
Front Street and the War Memorial in 1922	60
Front Street from the north, 1999	60
Church Street in 1891	61
Church Street with a 1910 Sunbeam	61
Braco in 1898	62
Former Post Office, 1999	62
Present day Postmaster	64
Envelope sent from Braco in 1850	64
The former mill at Greenloaning	66
The sawmill on the Knaik as it was in 1950	66
The Old Mill on the Knaik in the 1890s	66
Front Street in 1898	68
Front Street in 1950	68
Front Street, 1999	68
Braco from the south around 1910	69
Braco Bowling Green and Gardens in the early 1900s	72
Braco Bowling Green and Clubhouse, 1999	72
Braco Bowling Club, early 1900s	73
Muir Homes estate, 1999	76

Preface

This brief account of the area now known as Ardoch Parish is a response to the view, expressed at a meeting in Braco to consider ways of marking the second millennium, that it would be useful to update the booklet *Sketches of Ardoch* by Alexander H. Anderson, a former headmaster of Braco School, published in 1933 and itself an update of another booklet with the same title published before the First World War. In attempting this task I have also been aware of another booklet *The Parish of Ardoch and The Village of Braco* by Daniel J. McIldowie which was published in 1981 to commemorate the bicentenary of Ardoch Church, and is largely a series of personal reminiscences.

I have tried as far as possible to go back to original sources, but inevitably I have also had to depend in some instances on the memories of some of the older residents in the village. I am grateful for the help given by former archaeological colleagues in Glasgow, Manchester, and Edinburgh Universities and to the Local History Officer of the Smith Art Gallery and Museum in Stirling. The old photographs of Braco and Greenloaning have been generously provided by Mr Robert Bomont from his extensive collection of old postcards, while the present-day views are from photographs taken by Mr Steve van der Walt. The aerial views of Braco are reproduced by kind permission of Ray Mitchell. The list of residents and former residents in the parish whom I have quizzed about the past, and who have given freely and willingly of their time, is too long to mention everyone by name, but I am grateful to them all.

Undoubtedly there will be those who, on reading this account, will feel that there are omissions, while others will disagree with some of it. The decision as to what to include and the responsibility for factual accuracy are entirely mine.

William C. Hutchison

overleaf:
**6" Ordnance Survey map of the parish, 1866.
(Reproduced by permission of
the Trustees of the National Library of Scotland)**

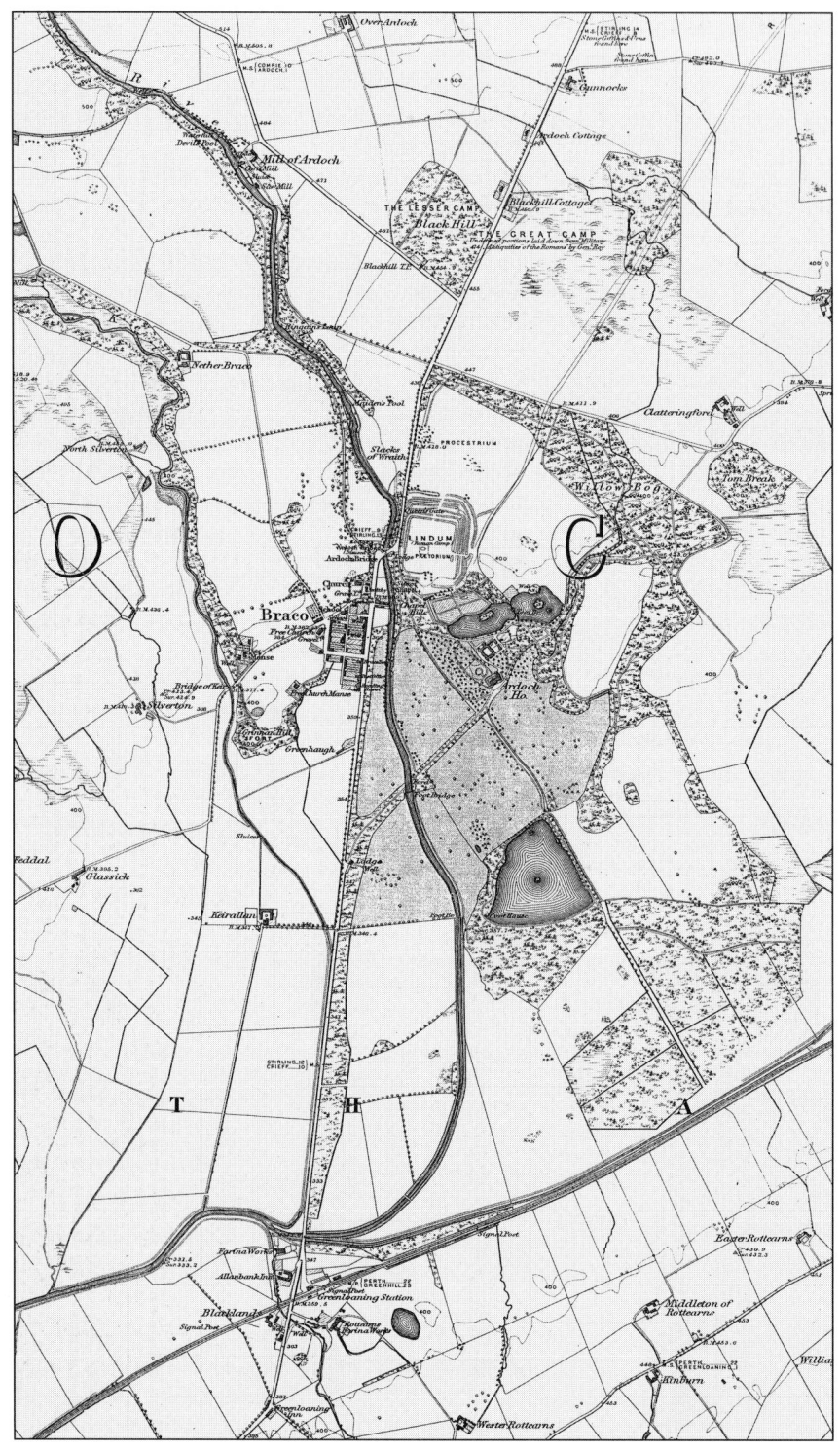

Introduction

Ardoch Parish as an area designated for civil or ecclesiastical purposes is relatively modern, having come into existence only in 1855. However, the name Ardoch has long been in use applied to the district which includes the Roman Fort, and the name is generally believed to mean 'the high place' being derived from the Gaelic 'ard' meaning 'high' and 'achadh', 'a field' or 'a place'. The derivation of the names of the two communities in the parish, Braco and Greenloaning, is not so clear. Braco has been the name of the castle for centuries, long before the village came into existence, and it has been suggested that it derives from the Gaelic 'bracach', 'a greyish place', which in turn derives from 'breac' meaning 'grey' or 'spotted', and 'achadh'. But then again 'breac' in Gaelic can also mean 'a trout', so perhaps in past times it was 'the place of the trout', though 'the grey place' seems to have the endorsement of the experts. It is interesting, however, to note that in County Fermanagh in Ireland there is a place called Breagho, whose name, pronounced similarly to that of our own village, is supposed to be derived from the Irish 'breagh mhath' meaning 'the wolf field', so there may well be other sources from which Braco could be derived. It is not clear when the name Greenloaning first appeared, although it is shown on Stobie's map of Perthshire published in 1782, and while the picturesque title of the present-day village would seem to suggest a reference to a green lane or green paddock, it is more likely that the name is derived from the Gaelic 'griannan loanan' meaning 'the sunny place on the marsh'. The same Gaelic root also occurs in of Grinnan Hill near Braco village.

Braco from the air in the 1980s.

Early History

Although the first writings relating to our area are concerned with the activities of the Romans in the first century AD, we can be sure that the history of man goes back well before that. A glance at the map of Scotland would suggest that as prehistoric man moved north following the ice age to colonise the land uncovered by the retreating ice, some tribes at least would cross the isthmus between Forth and Clyde at its eastern edge and move into what is modern day Perthshire. Although there are not many obvious signs in our parish of prehistoric man, standing stones – both monoliths and stone circles – are to be found close by, for example in the upper valley of the Machany Water, while the suggested origin of some of our place names may tell us of battles and rites in far off times.

Not surprisingly legends have come down to us which we may dismiss as myth, though it is often the case that such tales have some foundation in fact, even if the story has been modified and embellished over the years. One such tradition is that in days gone by the whole of what is now the valley of the River Allan was a large shallow lake. One day Helen, the local queen, was crossing this water, either by boat or, at a shallow stretch, on horseback, and was unfortunately drowned. The king was so distraught that he ordered the lake to be drained so that her body could be recovered. This was achieved by making a cutting at the southern end of the lake and this cutting is today where the Allan flows through a narrow passage just north of Kinbuck. The body of the queen was recovered and a mound raised over it. This mound can be found on today's maps as the Deaf Knowe about a mile north-west of Blackford. Indeed the place where the queen was attempting to cross became known as the Black Ford, hence the name of the present-day village. Truth or fiction, it is a good story, and it *is* known that when the Romans built their fort at Ardoch, the area to the south of the camp was described as a large marsh, resulting in a lesser need for fortifications on that side.

The Roman Fort at Ardoch from the north-east.

However, for more reliable written information we must turn to the Roman historian Tacitus who wrote a biography, sometimes partisan, of his father-in-law Agricola, who, while Governor of Britain, campaigned to subjugate the northern part of the country. Apparently the country south of the Forth–Clyde isthmus was brought under Roman control without too much difficulty and Agricola established a series of forts between the Firths of Forth and Clyde. As Tacitus writes:

> The narrow neck of land between Clota (Clyde) and Bodotria (Forth) was now secured by garrisons and the whole sweep of the country to the south was safe in our hands. The enemy had been pushed into what was virtually another island.

In AD 78 Agricola decided to move against the hostile tribes to the north and set out with a large army of some 30,000 men from one of his forts which was situated between modern day Camelon and Larbert. After crossing the swampy country bordering the Forth near Stirling using tree trunks lashed together, they camped at a place called Alauna which was probably near Dunblane, and from which, we may presume, the River Allan takes its name, though some may prefer the derivation from the Gaelic 'aluinn' meaning 'beautiful'. From there they marched on and established a marching camp beside the River Knaik at a settlement of the local tribe, the Damnonii, probably known as Lindum. Agricola pushed on northwards, leaving a cohort of 480 men to construct a more permanent fort. The main army ultimately fought a major battle at Mons Graupius in which the Caledonians were completely defeated with heavy losses. It used to be thought by some that this battle was fought not far from the Ardoch Fort at Dalginross near Comrie, but modern scholarship places it much further north with Mons Graupius being perhaps Bennachie in Aberdeenshire. Agricola was recalled by the Emperor Domitian in AD 84 or 85 before he could consolidate his victory and as a result, about AD 87, the Roman army withdrew from Scotland. The northern limit of Roman occupation became the strong stone wall erected between AD 120 and 130 from the River Tyne to the Solway Firth on the orders of the Emperor Hadrian.

The next Roman campaign in North Britain was under Governor Lollius Ubricus who certainly established a marching camp at Ardoch and rebuilt the fort. He also built the turf wall from Forth to Clyde named, for his Emperor, the Antonine Wall. Unfortunately he did not have a historian son-in-law like Agricola, so we do not have details of his campaign, though there is evidence that he constructed a new, smaller fort at Ardoch within the existing one. This resulted in extra rows of ditches and ramparts round the fort. Twice in the second half of the second century the Antonine Wall was breached by the hostile native tribes and the Romans withdrew to the south. Early in the third century, however, around AD 208 or 209 the Roman army returned under the Emperor Severus who rebuilt Hadrian's Wall and made several expeditions to the north, hoping to complete the conquest of Britain. Though he died in AD 211 before he could achieve his objective, it is likely that he used the fort at Ardoch and established marching camps which

The ditches of the Roman Fort at Braco.

show up on aerial photographs. After his day the Romans did not return and the Ardoch Fort was abandoned.

There are other evidences of the Roman occupation in the parish. The Roman road which ran north from Camelon to Strageath passed by the eastern edge of the Ardoch Fort to the small fort of Kaims Castle – or Camps Castle as it is described in earlier accounts – situated about 2¼ miles north-north-east of Ardoch. This fortlet, which is easily seen from the Braco to Muthill road where it crosses the Muir of Orchil at its highest point can be found across the road from the entrance to Orchil House. It consists of a rectangular rampart surrounded by circular earthworks, which may indicate that it was an earlier hill fort taken over by the Romans. A flag pole erected in the nineteenth century in the centre of the fortlet now lies on the ground and is much decayed. Further south, about half a mile north of the Auchterarder road there are the remains of a watch tower hidden from view in woodland, while another small fort is to be found about half a mile from the Old House of Orchil and just under a mile south-east from Kaims Castle. However, perhaps the most important outpost from the Ardoch Fort is to be found on Grinnan Hill on the other side of Braco village from the fort. Once again there are indications that this may have been an earlier fort taken over and fortified by the Romans. Although trees have today obscured the outlook somewhat, it is clear that it occupied a commanding position.

In the Greenloaning area another watchtower was detected by aerial photography in 1985 behind Greenloaning Farm, and excavation showed it to have been a rectangular tower surrounded by two circular ditches. On the other side of the road, beside Millhill Drive, the access road to Strathallan Park, a mound with associated earthworks is visible and this has been thought by some to be another Roman outpost. However, although it has not been excavated, current archaeological opinion is that it is pre-Roman and probably a Bronze Age burial mound or barrow. Across the A9 on Quoigs Farm, and clearly visible from the flyover, there is a tree-covered mound or motte known as The Roundel which is presumably later than the Roman period. A carved stone from here, known as the Roundel Stone, is in the custody of the Smith Art Gallery and Museum in Stirling, but is now thought to be a forgery. It can be seen outside the front of the building to the left of the main entrance.

The Dark Ages and the Medieval Period

The period between the withdrawal of the Romans and Scotland becoming a united kingdom is usually referred to as the Dark Ages because we have so little detailed information about it. However, although we do know that prehistoric man grew some cereals, as agriculture developed 'ferm touns' arose where between four and eight families joined together to work the land. Also during this period Christianity was introduced to Scotland, and probably St Blane who established the Celtic or Columban Church at Dunblane at the beginning of the seventh century and St Fillan who operated principally in Strathfillan and Strathearn in the early eighth century would be most likely to have had an influence on our area, though there is a strong tradition that, at an earlier time, St Patrick, who came to Scotland as a fugitive at the age of twenty-two in the mid-fifth century was active in the Muthill area. Near Blairinroar there was a chapel and two holy wells dedicated to St Patrick, that at Straid reputed to be excellent for whooping cough, while at Struthill, south of Muthill there was another St Patrick's Well recommended for the relief of lunacy! Another evidence of St Patrick's presence in the area may be the farm of Dalpatrick – Patrick's Field – at Strageath, and it is on record that the inhabitants of Muthill used to observe St Patrick's Day as a holiday. These early Christian clerics established churches, and although the Celtic Church did not build the lasting stone churches and cathedrals which later we associate with the Roman Church, they did have churches of humbler structure and round these churches grew up settlements, the forerunners of our towns and villages. Later when the Roman Church displaced the Celtic Church with the active help and approval of such rulers as Queen Margaret and King David I, more permanent stone structures arose such as we see today in the square tower of the old church at Muthill and the lower part of the tower of Dunblane Cathedral.

At this time we also have the arrival, by royal invitation, of Anglo-Norman aristocratic families who were given lands by the monarch, and so the feudal system came to Scotland with barons as overlords of most of the communities. One of the essential features of such communities was a mill, and, in addition to the small amount of arable land – the infield – close to the settlement and cultivated on a communal basis, there was also a moor or area for common grazing. Although Braco did not exist at this time, it is thought that the Muir of Orchil was such an area of common pasture for Muthill and perhaps for Blackford as well. In due course the settlement would be centred on a castle, the residence of the baron, and the settlement might include many ferm touns with more specific names like 'milton', kirkton', and the typically Scottish 'the mains' which was the ferm toun of the baron or 'lord of the manor' – the home farm.

The Seventeenth and Eighteenth Centuries

After the departure of the Romans no further mention is made of Ardoch Fort until the seventeenth century, though one can assume that the presumably sparse population continued to pursue their normal occupations of hunting, fishing, and farming. We have noted too the appearance on the scene of local lairds or landowners and mention of Ardoch Fort occurs in a letter written in 1672 by the laird of Drummond Castle, Lord Drummond, whose family had been granted the lands in the early eleventh century. In it he refers to the discovery of a gold ring and a great hoard of coin, presumably Roman, which two men had found within five miles of Drummond Castle 'amongst the hills which lie at its back', and goes on to describe the ditches and ramparts of the fort, but he notes, incidentally, that to the north-east they are not so marked for 'the ground being much better has made the people, against my grandfather's orders, till them down in some places'. He goes on:

> There was . . . a round opening like the mouth of a narrow well, of great depth, into which my grandfather ordered a malefactor to go, who (glad of the opportunity to escape hanging) went and brought up a spur and buckler of brass, which were lost the time a garrison of Oliver's (Oliver Cromwell's) dispossessed us of Drummond. There was found a stone there upon which was cut an inscription to show that a captain of the Spanish Legion died there. I shall copy it for you. It is rudely cut.

The stone in question is now in the Hunterian Museum of the University of Glasgow and the inscription has been translated, 'To the shade of Ammonius Damio of the First Cohort of the Spanish Stipendaries, who served for twenty seven years, his heirs have erected this monument'. The malefactor who had retrieved the stone was sent down again, but it is recorded that 'he expired in the foul air'.

In 1690 another criminal, who had been condemned by the baron court of a neighbouring lord, upon being promised a pardon, agreed to be let down into what was described as a hole on one of the sides of the praetorium 'which went downwards in a sloping direction for many fathoms, in which it was generally believed, treasures as well as Roman antiquities might be found'. The man was lowered down on a rope and brought up 'from a great depth' Roman spears, helmets, fragments of bridles, and several other articles. In the belief that further treasure remained to be found, he was lowered down for a second time, but he too fell victim to the foul air and died. The articles recovered were taken to Ardoch House but were all carried off by soldiers in the Duke of Argyll's army after the Battle of Sheriffmuir in 1715 and nothing more was ever heard of them.

Several other writers about this time commented on the finds at Ardoch. Lord Drummond later became the fourth Earl of Perth and had as his family physician Sir Robert Sibbald who had good opportunities to visit Ardoch. In one of his writings, in 1695, Sibbald refers to the stone recovered as having been 'taken up out of the Praetorium . . . below which there are caves'. This stone is also referred to by a Rev. Thomas who visited Ardoch in 1725 with Lord Oxford and said that it was to be seen in the garden wall at Drummond Castle. It is also recorded that an engraving of the stone appears on Adair's map of Strathearn published in 1720 and that it was presented by Sir Henry Stirling of Ardoch to the Lord Drummond who had organised the descent of the first condemned man, and that, after it had been kept at Drummond Castle for a while (presumably built into the garden wall), his grandson, who wrote the letter in 1672 already referred to, arranged for it to be sent to the University in Glasgow. Several other people visited the fort and commented on it or left sketches of what it was like. These included Alexander Gordon in 1726, Sir John Clerk of Penicuik in 1749, Richard Pococke, Bishop of Meath, in 1760, and Thomas Pennant in 1772. In addition, General William Roy, who was involved in the military survey of Scotland after the Jacobite Rising of 1745 and who produced the first large scale map of the whole of Scotland, visited the camps in 1755 and made an accurate plan which showed the ramparts on the south side of the fort and round the large marching camp immediately to the north in better condition than they are today. Indeed the *Old Statistical Account* of Scotland, published in 1791–1799 does say that the ramparts were steadily disappearing under the plough. However it is on record that the proprietor of Ardoch House had the whole of the middle camp enclosed with a stone wall to prevent such a misfortune in the future.

Reference has already been made to the fact that the hole from which various Roman relics were reputed to have been recovered was beside the praetorium. Within the main fort near the centre one can readily distinguish the outline of what has been a rectangular building long believed to have been the general's quarters or praetorium. However, this may instead be the remains of a hospice and burial ground associated with a medieval chapel shown on earlier maps as located to the east of the present entrance to Ardoch Estate in an area called Chapel Hill. Although a stone coffin was found near the site of the chapel, the other burials discovered were in wooden coffins which would not have been used in Roman times. The chapel belonged to Inchmahome Priory in the Lake of Menteith and was known as Chapel Raith meaning 'the Chapel of the Mound'. Nevertheless, whatever the function of the central rectangular building, the earlier accounts of a sloping pit beside it and Sibbald's statement that there are caves below it, link with the old story that a subterranean passage linked the fort with the outpost on Grinnan Hill. However unlikely this may seem to be, there is an old rhyme which goes back to time immemorial which runs:

> Between the Roman camp at Ardoch
> And the Grinnan Hill of Keir
> Lie nine kings' ransoms
> For nine hundred years.

Some versions have only seven kings' ransoms (or rents) for seven hundred years, but whatever the reputed size of the treasure no evidence for it has ever been found. Indeed the site of the hole is not known, for in 1720 a gentleman who rented Ardoch House while the proprietor was in Russia had the hole closed by a millstone and covered with a considerable depth of earth to prevent the escape of hares running into it with the loss of his pursuing dogs, and it cannot now be found. When the fort was excavated at the end of the nineteenth century one or two pits seven or eight feet in diameter were revealed near the centre of the camp, but though the shafts appeared to be deep they were not investigated because of the cost of shoring up the sides, and certainly no millstone was found. Of course there may be valuable relics to be found, for the evidence suggests that Ardoch was abandoned in a hurry so valuables may have been hidden in the expectation that they could be recovered when the fort was re-occupied, something which of course did not happen. It has been suggested that the shaft, rather than being a subterranean passage to Grinnan Hill, was either merely a store or else led under the river where filtered water could be collected.

Before leaving our account of the Ardoch Fort, mention should be made of the visit on 13 September 1842 of Queen Victoria and Prince Albert who had been staying at Drummond Castle. In her *Journal* the Queen relates:

> We came to a very extraordinary Roman encampment at Ardoch, called the 'Lindrum' (*sic*). Albert got out; but I remained in the carriage, and Major Moray showed it to him. They say it is one of the most perfect in existence.

The visit was not unexpected, and Major William Moray Stirling of Ardoch House made a special entrance into the fort consisting of two stone pillars surmounted by an arch bearing the initials V and A, and a wrought iron gate was fitted. The pillars and arch survived into the 1930s when the arch was lowered and built into the wall where it remains to this day.

Finally a strange tailpiece. In his book *Perthshire in History and Legend* A.C. McKerracher, the Dunblane local historian, states that when the house of Gunnocks just north of Braco was being renovated in the 1950s several photographs taken during the renovation were found on development to contain the figure of a Roman legionary. Mr McKerracher was given this information by the late Mr Carrick Anderson who was professionally involved in the renovation.

Roads and Bridges

Although the Roman road passed to the east of the present road from Greenloaning to Braco, probably crossing the Knaik downstream from the present bridges, in post-Roman times a road of sorts followed the line of the present road, crossing the Knaik by the so-called pack-horse bridge which is just inside the entrance to the present-day Lodge Park. This bridge, though thought by many to be of Roman origin, was built around 1430 by Michael Ochiltree who was Bishop of Dunblane as well as Dean of Muthill. No doubt he found the bridge useful when he travelled between the two centres, when, incidentally, he would also cross the Machany by the other bridge he built, still known today as Bishop's Bridge. Ochiltree's bridge over the Knaik was narrow, being only some six feet wide, but later an additional structure, three and a half feet wide, was attached to the older bridge and bound on by iron bands. A crevice developed between the two parts, and finally, in 1896, the additional part broke away and fell into the river. Meanwhile, the building of a new bridge had been started in 1861, but when the arch was almost completed, the supporting wooden framework collapsed and everything fell into the river, necessitating a fresh start. The new bridge,

The pack-horse bridge over the River Knaik with the 1862 bridge.

Cataracts on the River Knaik.

which carries the present-day A822 across the Knaik was finally finished in 1862. The old bridge of Bishop Ochiltree fell into disrepair, but was renovated in 1989 by the Association for the Protection of Rural Scotland at the instigation of the local Community Council.

This was not, however, the first time repairs to the bridge had been necessary. The Quarter Session minutes of March 1738 reported that an inspection was to be made of work carried out by Patrick Drummond, mason, Braco to repair the bridge 'to report if work is finished and sufficient'. Not until the minutes of March 1740 is it reported that Patrick Drummond had submitted an account for repairs to the bridge. Haldane of Gleneagles objected to payment since the work, in his view, was not satisfactory. Reports are minuted of several subsequent inspections of the bridge, for example by Lord George Murray on 17 May 1743, and presumably Patrick Drummond was ultimately paid. Two years after inspecting the bridge, Lord George Murray was the general accompanying Bonnie Prince Charlie on his march south.

The same Quarter Session minutes noted, in October 1736, that the road between the bridge over the Allan and Bridge of Ardoch 'has been considerably amended by the voluntary services of the people in the adjacent places' but that further work was needed to carry the water off the road which is in 'flat and morass ground' rendering it prone to flooding. Tools which it was authorised to purchase for this purpose were also to be used to repair the road from Crieff to Muthill and from Muthill to Bridge of Ardoch. The road was finally made properly in 1741–1742 as part of the great system of roads throughout the Highlands begun by General Wade after the 1715 Jacobite Rising, but its construction was not in fact undertaken by Wade, the work being carried out by General Clayton, the inspector being Edward Caulfeild (whose name is often erroneously spelt 'Caulfield'). The road followed a straight line north after bridging the Knaik, but in time a new road which offered easier gradients was constructed diverging from the military road at the present Garrick Cottage. This new road followed the route which was presumably that taken before the construction of the military road, for example by Bishop Ochiltree if he used both of his bridges.

Yet another bridge across the Knaik was constructed in the middle of the nineteenth century. This allowed access to the policies of Ardoch Estate when approaching from the south. The site of this bridge is clearly visible beside the northeast corner of the sewage works. Although there were earlier footbridges giving access to Ardoch Estate – one slightly downstream from the site of the bridge being discussed, and one opposite the lake which lies about half a mile south of Ardoch House – before the construction of the vehicular bridge, the river had either to be forded or else a detour made round by the bridge further up the river. The fording of the river was often impossible and sometimes dangerous, especially after heavy rains, since the river frequently rises with alarming rapidity and carries everything before it with irresistible force. The first bridge was built with a central pier, but it caused so many problems by intercepting trees and bushes washed down when the river was in spate that it was replaced by a single-span iron girder bridge sixty four feet wide resting on concrete piers built into the banks. This bridge lasted until 1936 when it too was demolished by a large tree brought down by the river after torrential rain. It was not replaced, although during the Second World War the army, who were camped in Ardoch Estate, erected a temporary Bailey Bridge.

Church Street (then known as Back Street) in 1898. The building on the left is the so-called Free Church School. See *page 27*.

The Development of the Village

The eighteenth century witnessed notable changes in the make-up of society, even if these were perhaps not so far-reaching as those that were to characterise the following two centuries. On the one hand the development of a moderately comprehensive road system meant that communication between different parts of the country became easier, while on the other, improvements in agricultural practice led among other things, to a redistribution of the populace. The ferm touns and the runrig method of cultivation began to disappear as fields were enclosed and consolidated farms were created. Trees were planted, oxen were replaced by horses for ploughing, and the encouragement by at least some of the landowners of draining, liming, fallowing, and rotation of crops led to better yields. While by present-day standards the number of people employed in agriculture was high, it is also true that the improvements led to greater efficiency and a consequent loss of rural population with people migrating to the growing towns. Many of those who remained in the country and who were employed either in agriculture or on the local estates also developed weaving as a cottage industry. Prior to the nineteenth century development of mills for weaving, Blackford was an important weaving centre, but nearby in our own parish there was a weaving community where the farms of Buttergask, Netherton, and Topfold are situated.

The century from 1745 onwards saw the development in Scotland of a number of planned villages, and in 1815 the village of Braco was feued mainly on land belonging to Braco Castle estate, the proprietor then being James Masterton, though the small development on the east side of the

Braco from the north in the early 1890s showing the smiddy on the right, while at the corner of Feddal Road the Toll House juts out over the pavement.

military road, where Waterside is today, was on Ardoch Estate. Since most of the new village was on Braco Castle land, it was given the name of 'Braco', though the minister of Muthill, writing in the *New Statistical Account* in 1837, expresses the view that 'Ardoch' would have been a preferable name. In this connection it is interesting to note that itinerant tinkers, or travelling people, used always to refer to the village as 'Brig o' Ardoch'. When the land was feued the main development was the building of houses on the west side of the road, later called Front Street. Behind these houses there were several wells, one of which, known as the Green Well, was located in the common bleaching and drying green in the area south of Smiddy Brae and west of Mid Lane. Another known as the Big Well was situated to the north of Smiddy Brae and east of Mid Lane and used to give a plentiful supply of water. Steps led down to facilitate the collection of water, but this source of water dried up unexpectedly, the water having presumably found a means of escape through the gravelly subsoil. The site of the well was covered over, but recently when the area was cleared and grassed over the site was discovered, and although the well has not been opened up, the wet, muddy patch in the grass gives away its location. A major source of water for the village was from the Knaik which was led into a lade behind the present Bridgend houses and fed a deep well behind the former Ardoch Inn, now the private house known as Ardochlea. At one stage this water was pumped up to a storage tank in the steading road. Although the lade was covered over by prisoners of war during the Second World War, the entrance to the lade can still be seen behind the north end of the Bridgend houses.

Ardoch Church, 1999.

The Churches

Reference has already been made to the probable existence of a medieval chapel located within the Roman Fort. Such a pre-Reformation church would of course have been Roman Catholic and there is a tradition that another Roman Catholic chapel existed in the past near the former Coupans Farm which is now run as boarding kennels and a cattery. Otherwise there are no records of Roman Catholic places of worship in the parish.

The Presbyterian church in Braco was built in 1780 as a Chapel of Ease, so called because it was meant to facilitate worship for those who lived at some distance from the parish church, located at that time in Muthill. The first minister was inducted on 25 March 1781. In May 1834 the church became a *quoad sacra* parish church and in February 1855 with the final establishment of the Parish of Ardoch as completely separate from Muthill Parish it became a *quoad omnia* parish church. Interestingly, since the church pre-dates the development of the village, it is known as Ardoch Church, not Braco Church.

Several alterations have been made to the church over the years. In 1862 the galleries on the north and south sides were removed and some of the windows on the south side were built up. The church was closed for four months while these alterations were carried out and was reopened for public worship on 24 August 1862, the sermon being preached by the Rev. George Alexander of Stirling. It was recorded that:

> the church is now one of the neatest and most comfortable in the Presbytery. Internally, it is altogether fitted up anew. The

Ardoch Church in 1910.

pulpit, instead of being in the centre of the church as formerly, is placed at the east end, and on each side of it is a stained glass window, put in at the suggestion of Mr George Kellie McCallum of Braco Castle.

Some thirty years later further alterations were carried out including the provision of an entrance vestibule and a choir chancel. Since then refurbishment and redecoration have been carried out on several occasions, electric light being installed after the Second World War, together with a sweet-toned pipe organ. For a period the organist was Jim McLeod who later achieved fame with his Scottish Dance Band. In 1985 a new church hall was added, connected to the rest of the building.

The ministers of Ardoch up to the present are as follows:

Chapel of Ease, 25 March 1781:
Rev. David Simpson	1781–1788
Rev. George Erskine	1788–1792
Rev. George Logan	1793–1802
Rev. Laurence Millar	1803–1812
Rev. Thomas Young	1813–1823
Rev. John MacFarlane	1823–1833

Quoad Sacra Parish, 31 May 1834
Rev. Alexander Oswald Laird	1833–1839
Rev. Samuel Grant	1840–1843

Quoad Omnia Parish, 21 February 1855
Rev. David Bonallo	1849–1858
Rev. John Robert Campbell	1858–1864
Rev. William Mair	1865–1869
Rev. Charles MacGregor	1869–1874
Rev. George Donald MacNaughton	1874–1903
Rev. Alexander Coskery	1904–1924
Rev. Lachlan MacPherson	1925–1928
Rev. James Hamill Maconnachie	1928–1929
Rev. Thomas Blackwood	1929–1934
Rev. John Young Miller	1935–1945
Rev. James Wright Wilson	1946–1953
Rev. C. Raymond Vincent	1953–1959
Rev. James Hosie	1959–1965
Rev. Iain R. Munro	1965–1968
Rev. Dugald McKinnon	1969–1982
Rev. Hamish Hepburn	1983–1991
Rev. Hazel Wilson	1991–

In 1843, the year of the Disruption, the minister, the Rev. Samuel Grant along with several members of the congregation seceded to form Braco Free Church. A new church was built in 1844 and opened on 5 January 1845, the congregation having in the meantime worshipped in a tent on the Bog Green which was where the present Village Hall now stands. A manse was built in

Greenloaning Manse in 1908.

1849. The Free Church people were interdicted from burying in the parish churchyard and so created a new burial ground beside the new church. The Free Church was distinguished by a tall spire but this was struck by lightning on Friday, 26 June 1874 and badly damaged while the Church itself suffered some damage from falling stones. The day it happened was a Fast Day and the congregation were about to assemble for a service. The headmaster of Braco School, Mr James G. Cuthbert, provides a colourful description of the incident in the school log-book:

> A flash of lightning struck the spire of the Free Church. Descending along the iron finial it exploded at its foot, 9 feet down in the solid masonry, and scattered the stones within a radius of 20 yards. Some of these in their descent riddled the roof of the Church. The electric fluid thereafter seems to have got divided into many streams, which sought the earth in all directions, some rending the steeple right down, others traversing the roof of the Church, and many passing through the building in a westerly direction, escaping through holes in the windows and through the walls. Had the accident happened three quarters of an hour later, lives would have undoubtedly been lost.

The damage was repaired and a new public clock, paid for by public subscription, together with a bell gifted by Mr John White of Hollybank, Stirling who was born in Braco in 1828, were placed in the tower. The church was demolished in the 1920s by the local authority but the clock tower minus the steeple was left standing.

In 1758, when Greenloaning was still part of the Parish of Dunblane, a church had been erected there. This came into the possession of the United Presbyterian Church, and at the celebration of its centenary in 1858:

a most appropriate sermon was preached by Dr Eadie, one of the professors of divinity of the United Presbyterian Church . . . and in the evening a soiree was held presided over by the Rev. J. Macintyre, the minister of the congregation.

It was reported that the company included 'some few, who had been baptised in the church, or had formerly been members of the congregation, coming distances from ten to twenty miles'. On the union of the U.P. and Free Churches in 1900 it joined up with Braco Free Church to form Braco United Free Church, and in 1905 the Rev. Thomas Blackwood became its minister. He appears to have been popular and to have had a successful ministry, and when in 1929 the union of the Church of Scotland and the United Free Church took place, it was agreed that Mr Blackwood be appointed minister of the united charge. Among other things it was also agreed that the manse of Ardoch should be the manse of the united charge and that the property of the Ardoch and Braco and Greenloaning congregations should become the property of the united congregation. In time the membership of the Greenloaning Church declined to the point where it was decided to close the church, all services being held in Ardoch Church, which much later also became a united charge with Blackford. The church at Greenloaning is now a private house.

The Church Tower and houses in Feddal Road, 1999.

Schools

Although the village of Braco as such did not come into existence until 1815, there was obviously a reasonable population in the area, as witness the establishment of a church in 1780. In the *Old Statistical Account* published in the 1790s, the minister of Muthill Parish refers to the existence of a school 'lately built on the south side of the parish' (i.e. Muthill Parish) with 60 to 80 pupils, the schoolmaster being the precentor at the Chapel of Ease. He is said to have 'a small salary, but chiefly depends on the profits of his school'. Nearly half a century later, after the village had been established, the then minister of Muthill, wrote of Ardoch in the *New Statistical Account*:

> Besides a prosperous church, they have also a prosperous school. A hundred children are well instructed there, in the common branches of learning. The schoolmaster's income arises altogether from the school fees, which doubtless should be otherwise.

He also refers to 'another school, where a very few children are taught, about a mile to the north of the village, and which has attached to it £2 a year of endowment, left by the Rev. William Hally, a former minister of Muthill', but there is now no evidence of the whereabouts of this school.

Whatever the earlier history of schools in the area may be, it seems that a school on the present site in Feddal Road was in existence by the 1830s. In addition, in the nineteenth century there existed in the corner of the present playground, at the junction of the Feddal Road with Church Street, a dame-school, apparently with a house for the teacher. Although this school was referred to as the Free Church School, this title arose simply because of its proximity to the Free Church, it having been erected by public subscription. It had, in the 1870s, the distinction of possessing the highest paid female teacher in Scotland! With the passing of the Education Act of 1872 the independent status of this school appears to have changed, and in 1879 a meeting of the Braco School Board was held to consider the proposed union of the two schools. This proposal apparently caused some concern to the headmaster of the village school, Mr J.G. Cuthbert, who, wrote in the school log in 1888 with reference to another meeting of the Board which wanted to divide the pupils but had still failed to reach a decision on the proposed union:

> The folks have taken it into their heads that an amalgamation between the village schools is inevitable, the juniors to be taught in the 'other' school, the seniors here. The 'Board' has gathered statistics to effect this or something like it. Such a union is clearly unnecessary in every respect.

He goes on to complain that urgent needs for books and maps, and the repair of the school desks are having to take second place to the unnecessary arguments about plans to divide the pupils between the two schools. Ultimately, however, the 'other' school seems to have been demolished along

The children of Greenloaning Primary School, 1947, with some little brothers and sisters too young to attend.

The children of Greenloaning School, 1999.

with the teacher's house which jutted out into the roadway, and all pupils were taught together.

A perusal of the school log-books provides an interesting commentary on a number of aspects of life in Braco over the last century and a quarter. There are many comments on the weather which frequently had a major effect on the life of the school, heavy snow in winter blocking country roads and making it impossible for pupils to attend. Less frequently there are complaints about oppressive heat. Records of the illnesses which kept pupils off school make one realise how, in addition to colds and influenza, there were prevalent such ailments as measles, chickenpox, scarlet fever, mumps, diphtheria, and, on at least one occasion, typhoid. On occasion the school had to be fumigated following on an outbreak of an infectious disease. Mr Cuthbert, who was headmaster until 1897, appears to have waged a constant battle with parents who would not accept the necessity of sending their children to school and who kept them off when it suited them. The pupils too seem to have felt they had the right to help with harvesting or to act as beaters for local shooting parties whenever they wished, to the annoyance of the headmaster who complains that a few farmers seem to find it cheaper to employ juvenile labour than that of adults. All these absences clearly affected the educational process, and in a heartfelt entry in 1875, Mr Cuthbert writes, 'The cultivation of intelligence is a most exasperating labour', and again, in 1879, his sole entry for one week is 'Beginning to feel fagged. Wish for the holidays.' Nevertheless, he gave the pupils a half-holiday when there was a local curling match on one of the Ardoch ponds, but his concern for their moral welfare is apparent in the entry for 5 April 1878 which reads: 'Noticed boys and girls play together at skipping rope. Heard on Thursday stories of lads and lasses kissing. Stopped this communion of play.'

His successor, Mr J.B. MacOwan, continues to be concerned about absences for harvesting, potato lifting, or beating, and he puts a ban on such absences by the younger children, but in 1901 official potato holidays lasting for three weeks appear to have been instituted. While in 1921 the School Board decided to restrict the break to six days, it was later extended to two weeks. In 1905 the report of H.M. Inspector recommends the provision of a piano, but the recommendation was apparently not acted upon, for eight years later, in 1913, the inspector reported that 'singing might be more tuneful if a piano were provided'. An earlier report had pointed out that as the pupils had the advantage of a neighbouring common to play on, part of the school playground might be turned into a school garden, and some four years later the garden was inspected and it was reported that:

> the garden is in good condition, and affords scope for instruction in all branches of horticulture. A frame is provided by means of which plants are raised from seed. Six sets of tools are provided for four plots. There are eight boys. . . . Plots of grasses and other agricultural plants are also provided, as well as plants unusual in the district.

The old school and schoolhouse, Greenloaning, with Greenloaning farmhouse in the background, probably photographed in the early years of the twentieth century.

The boys were said to be taking up garden work at their own homes, and 'entering into healthy rivalry with the school garden'.

Oddly enough little mention is made of national or international events which must have had some effect on school life. There is no mention of, for example, the Golden Jubilee of Queen Victoria, of her death or that of Edward VII, though later the death of George V is recognised by a service in Ardoch Church. The outbreak of the First World War occurred during the school summer holiday but it is noted that on 23 October 1915 soldiers who were marching from Aberuthven to Larbert were billeted overnight in the school. Right up to the start of the Second World War, Empire Day appears to have been celebrated every May with the Union Jack being flown until sunset.

After the end of the First World War things began to change. In December 1920 it was agreed that children from the country could be provided with hot cocoa during the dinner hour. In 1924 permission was given for the school to erect a wireless receiving set and the following month 'wireless lectures' commenced with the pupils listening to Professor Rait of Glasgow University talking on Sir William Wallace. They also 'heard noises from the London Zoo very distinctly and were greatly interested'.

The school log records that at the beginning of March 1921 the school cleaner demanded a payment of ten shillings per week which was apparently refused, for her resignation is noted on 1 April. Perhaps, however, the Board relented for her reinstatement is noted on 22 April! Thanks to the generosity of Mr and Mrs Muir of Braco Castle, school picnics were held in the grounds of the Castle and at the Christmas party held in the Village Hall, each pupil received a box of chocolates from Mrs Muir. Complaints must have been made about the warmth, or lack of it, in the classrooms for in 1930 the log contains tables showing the outside temperature each day together with

The new school at Greenloaning, 1999.

the temperatures recorded in each of the classrooms. In January the outside temperature varied from 31 °F to 46 °F while the classroom temperatures varied from 42 °F to 58 °F. In February it varied from 26 °F to 44 °F outside and from 40 °F to 56 °F indoors. March produced similar figures, and representations must have been made to those in authority for by the following September central heating had been installed. The furnace for the system was in a classroom and this may account for the fact that on 7 November the headmaster was off with suspected carbon monoxide poisoning. Happily he was back at work by the tenth. Fire drill was also instituted about this time with designated pupils having particular duties, one boy being responsible for running to the police station to give notice of the fire.

The police were called in September 1929 when the school had been broken into. Apparently the articles stolen were some pencils and a strap. There is no record of the culprit being found or whether the stolen strap was used to administer suitable punishment to the thief.

In 1939 some structural alterations were made to the school providing better staff accommodation and improved lavatories, and while this work was carried out pupils were accommodated in the Village Hall and the Church Session House. In this year too we have the first mention of pupils competing in the Perth Music Festival when a team of senior girls showed their skill at country dancing and were awarded second place in the rural class. Later entries in the log record the school choir gaining first place in the competition for 2- and 3-teacher schools, an achievement they repeated on at least two further occasions and gained not only an Honours Certificate but also the Challenge Cup.

Braco Nursery School, 1999.

Braco School, 1999.

Braco Primary School: Primary 1–4, 1999.

Braco Primary School: Primary 5–7, 1999.

Feddal Road around 1910 showing the schoolhouse, the school, the Free Church with its steeple, the Bog Green, where the Village Hall now stands, and, in the distance, the then Ardoch Church Manse.

The outbreak of the Second World War brought its problems. The school roll was greatly increased by the influx of children evacuated from Glasgow, and for a while the school operated a two-shift system, the evacuees being taught in the forenoon by teachers brought from Glasgow, while the Braco children plus some who had been privately evacuated were taught in the afternoon. Later the Braco children occupied the school full-time while the evacuees were taught in the Braco Hall and in the Church Session House. Another development occurred in 1941 when 43 Roman Catholic children arrived after the Easter holiday. They had with them their own teachers and a double shift system was instituted because of a shortage of desks. Later they were taught full-time in Braco Hall, but in March 1942 it was reported that the school had been reorganised allowing the complete integration of the Roman Catholic pupils with the rest of the school. A final war-time activity of the pupils is recorded in the same year when, on 30 September, 28 lbs. of rose hips which had been collected were sent off to the depot in Airdrie, while two days later another consignment of 26½ lbs. followed.

Braco School continues to thrive. In the last decade it has been enlarged by converting the headteacher's house into extra classroom accommodation which has been incorporated into the school. There is an active Parent-Teacher Association which ensures good co-operation between the school staff and the parents of the pupils, and continues to strive to raise funds for the benefit of the children. In the last year a new computer has been purchased and this was matched by the Education Authority who provided a second computer for the school. The School Board is fully complemented and works closely with the Parent-Teacher Association, the Education

Authority, and the school staff. Several members of the Parent-Teacher Association are also members of the School Board.

Another school, of course, existed at Greenloaning. Originally situated on the west side of the Crieff road just south of Greenloaning Farm, it was replaced in 1927 by a more modern building on the site which it now occupies. In recent years the number of pupils had dropped to a level which made the future of the school seem doubtful, but the school was nevertheless refurbished and it is to be hoped that the new houses being built at Greenloaning will result in an increased roll and ensure the future viability of the school. Both Braco and Greenloaning schools provide only primary education, pupils proceeding to either Crieff or Dunblane for their secondary education. Some attend Morrison's Academy in Crieff which is an independent school.

Hotels and Inns

While it is known that in the past several illicit stills existed in the remoter parts of the hills and moors in the parish, there were four legal establishments where liquor could be obtained. Braco Hotel, which was run by the Graham family for nearly ninety years, is still in existence, has recently been refurbished, and is run by Ken and Doris Coates. The other hotel in Braco was the Ardoch Inn which became a temperance hotel around 1920 when run by William Adam. Later it became more of a tearoom, and finally the private house known as 'Ardochlea'. In Greenloaning there is the Allanbank Hotel which has continued under its present owners Robin

Greenloaning Inn, Mary Ann's, in the 1890s. The signpost pointing up Mill Hill Road, which was then the main road to the north, records the mileages to Sheriffmuir, Blackford, Auchterarder and Perth.

Braco Hotel in the 1890s. Among other things, the road surface has changed markedly!

Ardoch Hotel (now the private house 'Ardochlea') in 1918. The proprietor's name, James Eadie, is above the door and the horse-drawn wagon is delivering mineral waters.

'Ardochlea', formerly the Ardoch Hotel, 1999.

Braco Hotel in Front Street around 1948. The hotel has a clock above the door. Front Street has telegraph poles on the one side and electricity poles on the other. The signs for the garage are in the distance while on the left the houses in Gentlecroft are under construction.

Braco Hotel, 1999.

Allanbank Hotel in the 1890s. The sign above the window in the gable-end reads 'Alanbank Hotel, Horses and Carriages on Hire'.

Allanbank Hotel, 1999.

The former Greenloaning Inn being renovated as a private house, 1999.

and Mandy Nisbet, and is a popular meeting place for several organisations. For many years another hostelry flourished on the east side of the Crieff road at the foot of Mill Hill Road. This was run for many years by Mary Ann Anderson and was always known as 'Mary Ann's', and even though it was closed in the 1970s the bend in the road is still referred to as 'at Mary Ann's'. There is a strong tradition that Robert Burns visited Mary Ann's, and in view of his appointment as an exciseman covering the Dunblane area, this could well be the case, but unfortunately no documentary evidence can be produced in support. The Greenloaning Burns Club was formed in Mary Ann's in 1889.

The Village Halls

The earliest village hall was the Polton Hall which was situated on the west side of Mid Lane north of Smiddy Brae where today there is a house called 'Poulton'. The Polton Hall was a two storey building and on the upper floor were held dances and other functions including the local Flower Show. The floor was reputed to be well sprung and excellent for dancing, but the ground floor was occupied by the vans of some of the local shopkeepers and stables for their horses and the consequent odours tended on some occasions to permeate to the upper floor. Another disadvantage was that the only exit, in case of fire, was by a single inward-opening door at the foot of the stair. This was pointed out by Mrs Muir of Braco Castle and may have influenced the decision by her husband, Mr J. Finlay Muir, to provide the village with

Another picture of Greenloaning Station in the 1920s with transport awaiting arriving passengers.

Greenloaning Station in more modern times.

a new, commodious public hall which was built on the old Bog Green in Feddal Road in 1926. The old Polton Hall has since been demolished, but the new hall is in regular use by many of the organisations in the village. In 1999 Jim Halley retired after many years of devoted service as hall keeper.

The Railway

One event which had a profound effect on the life of the parish was the arrival in 1848 of the railway with a station at Greenloaning. The Scottish Central Railway Company decided in 1844 to establish a railway line from Larbert through Stirling to Perth and the section from Stirling to Perth was opened on 23 May 1848. A proposal was also made in 1844 to provide a spur from Greenloaning to Crieff, but this had to be dropped because the local landowners would not make the necessary land available. A Goods Shed and a Station House were erected at Greenloaning, and in 1851 arrangements were made for a weekly grain market and consideration given to markets for stock, butter and cheese. The Scottish Central Railway Company and the Caledonian Railway Company amalgamated in 1865 becoming known simply as the Caledonian Railway. The 'Caley' in due course became part of the London, Midland and Scottish Railway in 1924. The L.M.S. in turn became part of British Rail which was split up in the 1990s into different companies, those passenger-carrying companies which today use the line through Greenloaning being ScotRail and the Great North

Allanbank Hotel and the entrance to Greenloaning Station in the early 1900s with the trees pulled over to form a decorative arch for a special occasion, possibly a Royal visit.

Eastern Railway (G.N.E.R.), though the station itself was closed to passenger traffic in 1956 and to goods traffic in the 1960s.

In its heyday Greenloaning was a busy station. Not only did it make it easier for people to travel to other towns and cities, but it was very busy with goods traffic. Both hotels in Braco operated horse-drawn wagonettes to convey passengers to and from the station, and many a race was had between the conveyances of the rival establishments as they vied for custom. Indeed the railway made it easy for people to come to Braco, which became a popular holiday resort, and the railway timetables showed the stop as 'Greenloaning for Braco'. The railway also provided employment, for, in addition to the stationmaster, there were usually three porters and three office staff, plus the signalmen and the squads whose job it was to maintain the track in good condition.

Coal and lime were carried in open wagons which were unloaded manually by shovel, but other commodities such as grain, fertilisers, feeding stuffs, seed potatoes and also cattle and sheep were loaded into vans. It was a common sight to see stock being walked along the road from Braco to the station at Greenloaning to be transferred into the appropriate trucks. Although no longer grown commercially in the parish, for some years raspberries were grown at Wester- and Mid-Rottearns by the firm of Calder and Watson providing another source of seasonal employment not only for the locals but also for people from the neighbouring towns. When production was at its height as much as four hundred tons of raspberries could be loaded on to the trains at Greenloaning in one season.

Greenloaning Station, 1999, now no longer in use.

The Principal Estates

The four principal estates in the parish were, in alphabetical order, Ardoch, Braco, Feddal, and Orchil, each of which had its mansion house or castle associated with it. In addition, Greenloaning was on the edge of Keir Estate but as most of that property, including Keir House, lies outwith our parish, it will not be dealt with here, and attention will be confined to the four principal estates already mentioned. Although Ardoch House and Feddal Castle have both been demolished, it is appropriate for this account of the parish to say something about all four.

Ardoch Estate was originally owned by the Sinclairs who had been given it by the Abbot of Lindores, but in the middle of the sixteenth century it came into the possession of William Stirling, a brother of Sir James Stirling of Keir, as a result of his marrying the heiress of the Sinclair family. This branch of the Stirlings continued in direct male succession for nearly three centuries. The fifth proprietor, Sir William Stirling, Bart., who died in 1702 was a minor when he succeeded to the title and the estate was managed by his uncle, Robert Stirling, who was known as 'The Tutor of Ardoch' and is reputed to have reached the great age of 112 when he died in 1716. The seventh laird, also Sir William, who is credited with building a new house in the immediate vicinity of the earlier mansion, also arranged for the enclosure of the Roman Fort to prevent further damage by ploughing. He had no male issue and was succeeded by his daughter who married Charles Moray of Abercairney, her son adopting the name of William Moray Stirling of Ardoch and Abercairney. He was succeeded in turn by his sister who married Henry Home Drummond of Blair Drummond and the estate passed first to her

Ardoch House in 1898.

The south entrance to Ardoch House in 1899, now the access road to the new cemetery.

The overgrown ruins of the south entrance gatehouse of Ardoch House in 1999.

The main entrance to Ardoch House showing the North Lodge, now demolished.

eldest son, George Stirling Home Drummond and then to a younger son, Charles Stirling Home Drummond Moray who in his name retained the names of all the proprietors since the sixteenth century. The Drummond Morays still retain the estate of Abercairney but Ardoch Estate is presently owned by Mohammed al Tajir of the United Arab Emirates. During the Second World War children evacuated from Glasgow were billeted in Ardoch House for a short period, and it also provided accommodation for members of the Women's Land Army. The house itself was demolished about ten years ago, but the ice houses are still there and some magnificent trees which are well over a hundred years old can still be seen, though access to the grounds, formerly enjoyed by the public, has been denied by the present owner.

In 1715 the Earl of Mar spent the night before the Battle of Sheriffmuir at the old Ardoch House, his army being encamped in the Roman Fort, and after that inconclusive battle the Duke of Argyll's forces paused in their pursuit of Mar's army to spend a night at Ardoch. We have already referred to the belief that the Roman artefacts recovered from a pit in the fort were taken to Ardoch House and their subsequent disappearance is certainly blamed on Argyll's men.

Just over a hundred years earlier, in the reign of Mary Queen of Scots, Ardoch House was the scene of exciting happenings. Marion Crichton, the daughter of Sir Robert Crichton of Clunie, the Lord Advocate, and a sister of the Admirable Crichton, was sent by her stepmother to her brother-in-law, Henry Stirling of Ardoch, 'with the view of advancing her education in such knowledge and accomplishments as befitted her rank and prospects in life'. Her stepbrother, Sir Robert Crichton, who wished to get his hands on Marion's fortune either by marriage or in some other way, resolved to kidnap her. Accompanied by some of his associates and forty armed horseman, they arrived at Ardoch House and claimed to be seeking the Earl of Bothwell who had been declared a rebel and a traitor. Not satisfied with being told that Bothwell was not in hiding in the house, they entered, stole several articles, and abducted Marion forcibly. Although we know that the raiders were subsequently caught and declared rebels there is no record of what happened to them, but Marion was recovered unharmed.

Braco Estate is an ancient one and was one of the possessions of the Grahams, the Earls of Montrose. The Castle was originally a square tower which was probably built no later than the sixteenth century. The house has been added to and modified over the years. In the seventeenth century Sir William Graham added an extension to the south and the roof was altered to link the two parts. This Sir William was the uncle of the famous Marquis of Montrose and was created Baronet of Braco in 1625. James Graham of Braco is listed as a private in Lieutenant General Drummond's troop mustered at Stirling on 18 September 1667, while a year later Sir William Graham of Braco was commissioned in No.6 Company of the Perthshire Militia. Cromwell is said to have stayed in the Castle in 1650, but whether by invitation or not is not clear. In the following century the sympathies of the Grahams of Braco were definitely with the Jacobites, and Jacobite forces garrisoned the Castle in 1716 but fled after the Battle of Sheriffmuir on the approach of the Duke of Argyll's men. At the time of the 1745 Rising the laird of Braco was General David Graham and with his death at the end of the eighteenth century Graham ownership of Braco came to an end. It seems that allegiance was now transferred to the House of Hanover for we find that the laird is equerry to George III. Believing that the monarch would

Braco Castle in 1922.

visit Braco Castle while on a visit to Scotland, he added a large L-shaped wing to the east, presumably to accommodate the king's retinue but also no doubt to impress the royal visitor with his own importance. As it turned out George did not come to Braco at all!

In the nineteenth century Braco Castle was owned by Lieutenant Colonel G.K. McCallum who was responsible for the modern layout of the garden and grounds although further additions were made in the early twentieth century. The two ponds beside the drive which approaches the Castle may be old fishponds relating to an earlier tower house. Today the Castle presents the appearance of a large but somewhat austere mansion. The various additions have been well blended together, but the building is conspicuously lacking in architectural decoration though there is, above a ground floor window to the left of the front entrance, a coat of arms, presumably a crest of the Grahams, carved in the stonework and much weathered.

In the nineteenth and twentieth centuries the owners of Braco Castle were closely associated with the life of the village. In 1861 G.K. McCallum established a Reading Room in the village and supplied it with books and newspapers, but it failed to attract much interest, and was ultimately closed. The next owner of the Castle, Sir William Renny Watson, gifted land to be formed into a Bowling Green to commemorate the Diamond Jubilee of Queen Victoria in 1897, at a nominal rent of 1d per annum. He also took a great interest in the Curling Club and in the village school.

After him, ownership of Braco Castle passed to Patrick Ness who re-established the Reading Room in 1902 in the old toll house which was

Braco Castle, 1999.

situated on the north side of Feddal Road at its junction with the Crieff road. It seems that this project enjoyed greater popularity than had been shown for the previous Reading Room, though whether this was for the reading material or for the draughts and dominoes which were available is debatable. After her husband's death Mrs Ness continued to take a great interest in the Reading Room until her own death in 1915, and left to it in her will a legacy of fifty pounds. Ultimately, however, this Reading Room, which had been moved to premises at the other end of the village also fell into disuse. The old toll house was ultimately demolished as it stuck out into the Crieff road beyond the line of the present pavement.

Braco Castle was bought in 1911 by F.A. Brown-Douglas, but after the end of the First World War ownership of the estate passed to J. Finlay Muir who, as has already been mentioned, defrayed the entire expense of providing the present Village Hall. In addition, Mr and Mrs Muir were much involved in the life of the school, and as well as permitting school picnics to be held in the Castle grounds and providing chocolates for each pupil at the Christmas party, already noted, they donated the Muir Cup for competition between the school houses and Mrs Muir was frequently asked to present the prizes at the end of the school session. The Muirs were keenly interested in the Castle gardens in which they grew daffodils for sale. The walled garden lies on a gentle south-facing slope to the west of the Castle and is reached by a path through a rhododendron shrubbery. Although one can imagine its former glory, it is now, to a large extent, uncared for and the magnificent range of glass houses against the north wall are in a dilapidated condition. One can only hope that some restoration may be possible at some future date.

In the early 1970s J. Finlay Muir's son, Commander Robin Muir, sold the Castle and its immediate policies, but continued to live in Silverton farmhouse and retained an interest in farming the estate, an interest still maintained by his son, Mr Nicholas Muir. The present owners of the Castle are Mr and Mrs M. van Ballegooljen.

Feddal Estate, like Ardoch, no longer has a mansion house, and has had a varied history. At one time the part known as Ardoch Feddal belonged to the Drummond Morays of Ardoch and Abercairney, but early in the twentieth century they sold off the Ardoch Feddal part of their lands. The laird of Feddal at that time was G.B. Thornton who was succeeded in 1911 by E. Pullar. During the First World War, Feddal was owned by J. Conchie who was erroneously suspected by some of being a German spy, and in 1922 the estate was sold in various lots. J. Finlay Muir of Braco Castle bought some lots to add to his estate, and Feddal Castle itself together with the Feddal Hill and the farms of Middle Feddal, Crofthead, and Whistlebrae were bought by Major J. Falconer Stewart who took a great part in village life. After the end of the Second World War it was decided to demolish the Castle.

The castle which was demolished was a nineteenth century building in the Scottish baronial style, built close to the old House of Feddal a portion of which still remained and was used as potting sheds and stores for the gardens. The older house was supposed to have been visited by Bonnie Prince Charlie when he was a fugitive after the Battle of Culloden, and the room in which he was said to have lain in hiding and the small hole in the wall through which food was passed to him used to be pointed out. It is generally accepted that Rob Roy was a frequent visitor to Feddal to have a game of cards with the laird, though the friendship was formed in a somewhat unusual way. It seems that the laird of Balhaldie was really one of the chiefs of the McGregors, though he had to change his name when the name McGregor was proscribed. However, as an erstwhile McGregor chief he was exempt from paying protection money to Rob Roy to prevent his cattle being stolen. Balhaldie was proud of his prowess as a swordsman,

Old Feddal House in 1898.

Feddal Castle in 1909.

Orchil House in 1898.

Orchil House, 1999.

and learning that the laird of Feddal also claimed similar expertise he sent a challenge to him. A duel took place which was fiercely fought, but in the course of it Feddal's sword blade snapped and, in a token of surrender, Feddal bared his breast for Balhaldie to administer the *coup de grace*. He however would have none of it as he recognised Feddal as a skilful swordsman and a brave man, and the two became firm friends. Feddal soon discovered that Balhaldie did not pay protection money to Rob Roy and decided that he would not pay either. This did not meet with Rob Roy's approval and he arranged one night for his men to steal all the stock of Feddal and his tenants. In the morning Feddal and his men set off to search for the cattle and met up with Rob Roy who said that he just happened to be in the neighbourhood. On hearing of the loss he said that if Feddal would resume paying protection money he thought that he might be able to recover the cattle, which, of course, he duly did. This was a salutary lesson to Feddal and others not to meddle with Rob Roy, and the two buried their differences and became firm friends.

The Barony of **Orchil** dates back to 1560 when the second Earl of Montrose settled the lands of Orchil and Rottearns on his third son Mungo Graeme. Originally the estate was very large, stretching from Auchterarder through Blackford to Rottearns and across the hill towards Comrie, but today the Old House of Orchil is a delightful small mansion house dating from the sixteenth century and sitting in its own 25 acres at the centre of the three hundred acre Orchil Estate.

James Graeme, the third laird, married Jean the daughter of Sir James Chisholme of Cromlix and a relation, albeit distant, of the wife of the William Stirling who acquired Ardoch Estate from the Sinclairs by marriage. The

The Old House of Orchil, 1999.

next laird, James Graeme married Lilias the daughter of Sir Laurence Oliphant of Gask, and so established a link between the House of Orchil and the House of Gask. David Graeme became the sixth laird in 1712 and in 1726 the Duke of Montrose tried to repossess the estate, but without success. Under David Graeme the House became known as a 'safe house' in the 1745 Rising, and later he formed, with five others, the Trust of Gask and bought back the House of Gask from the Crown after it had been confiscated. David's portrait was discovered by the present owners at a London auction in 1994 and, after restoration, it now hangs in the drawing room of the Old House of Orchil.

David Graeme's son William was the last Graeme to live at Orchil as he had no male heir and the property passed to his sister who had married the Dunblane architect James Gillespie who adopted the name of James Gillespie Graham. Gillespie Graham, who had trained with Nash in London, became a famous architect who designed many Gothic style castles and churches in Scotland including St Mary's Roman Catholic Cathedral in Edinburgh, St Andrew's Cathedral in Glasgow, and the Tolbooth Church in Edinburgh which occupies a commanding site at the top of the Lawnmarket looking right down the High Street. He was a town planner of some genius, his Moray Estate being the most imaginative and successful of the Edinburgh New Town schemes. He and A.W. Pugin competed for the design of the Palace of Westminster. They did not win, but Pugin had also entered with Charles Barry and they won. In the Old House of Orchil Gillespie Graham and Pugin designed the magnificent ceiling in the Chapel-Drawing Room which was probably the prototype for the Banner Hall ceiling in Taymouth Castle.

Ownership of the Old House of Orchil subsequently passed through various hands, the Rev. Thomas Crawford being the proprietor from just before the First World War until 1926. He gave a medal for a few years for the dux of Braco School and also donated the Crawford Cup for competition between Braco and Muthill Bowling Clubs. The House and also Orchil Home Farm were bought by the Jackson family who lived in the house until 1983 and still farm the estate. Eventually, in 1988, after it had been left unoccupied for five years the Donald family purchased it and have completely restored it.

There is, not far from the Old House of Orchil, another more modern house built in 1868, known as Orchil House. It was partially destroyed by fire in 1915 but was rebuilt.

John G. McKendrick – A Lad o' Pairts

A wander round an old churchyard sometimes reveals information about those who lived locally in times gone by, for the old headstones often tell us the occupations and occasionally other facts about those buried there. Equally, of course, one is sometimes left wondering about what is not revealed and often about what ultimately became of the sons and daughters whose name only is carved in stone. As Thomas Gray wrote in his 'Elegy Written in a Country Churchyard':

> Some mute inglorious Milton here may rest.

All this is true of both burial grounds in Braco, but it is perhaps worth telling a story which lies behind one tombstone in the Parish Church graveyard which records the death of James McKendrick, his wife, Margaret Faichney and some of their children and grandchildren. The stone is to be found near the eastern edge of the cemetery.

The McKendricks are said to have come from the Balquidder area, but after the Forty Five Rising, when the clans were scattered, they settled on the Feddal Estate. Several generations later, James McKendrick became the grieve or factor on Braco Estate, and his is the first name to appear on the tombstone. Of his children, John became a gardener and died at Gainsborough, while one of his sons, Henry, settled in Braco, married a Janet Eadie of Casmbushinnie, and had three children, James who was killed in a railway accident at Larbert when he was only nineteen years of age, Elizabeth who married John Thomson in Braco, and Christina who lived with her sister in Braco and died in 1941. John and Elizabeth Thomson's son, James McKendrick Thomson, a grandson of the Braco factor, was a vice-president of the Ardoch Curling Club.

However, Henry's older brother James is the one with whom we are most concerned. He was apprenticed to a draper in Stirling and afterwards set up business in Aberdeen, but things went wrong. His wife died and he moved to London where he contracted tuberculosis, finally returning to Braco to die. Just before his business in Aberdeen ran into trouble, his wife had given birth in 1841 to a son called John who, after his parents' deaths, was brought to Braco at the age of four to stay with his grandfather who by that time had retired from his post at Braco Castle and had built himself a little house in the village in the Feddal Road just opposite where the Free Church would be built. John had his early education at Braco School and in his autobiography which he wrote in later life, he says:

> I received the elements of a fair education in reading, writing, arithmetic, and the elements of grammar, with a dash of geography which interested me more than all the other subjects. Of course we were drilled in Bible knowledge. The school consisted of one room only and the boys and girls were in the same classes. We had the usual experiences of a village school, such as fighting, bathing in the Burn o' Keir, harrying wasps' nests with often direful consequences, or rabbit hunting.

At the age of thirteen years John was fee-ed to Andrew Brydie the farmer at Silverton to act for six months as a herd laddie, his duties being to look after the cattle in their wanderings over the pasturage. Very few areas of grass were fenced and it was necessary to prevent the cattle from straying on to the growing grain crops. For his six month's work he received the sum of one pound. He writes:

I was out in the open air all day from five in the morning until eight in the evening; the servant girl brought my porridge to me in the morning and my dinner at mid-day to a particular spot, and I had my supper when I returned home at night – another bicker of porridge and milk. All this strengthened my physique, and no doubt enabled me to enter upon a career of hard work in after years.

After finishing his schooling in Braco, where he seems latterly to have taken a great interest in learning, he was sent off in 1855 to Aberdeen to start an apprenticeship in an advocate's office. While there he continued his education by taking classes in his spare time, though he continued to spend his holidays at Braco where he became very interested in the animals and plants of the countryside. John ultimately abandoned the law office for the study of medicine and in 1864 graduated from the University of Aberdeen. After appointments in Chester and London, he obtained an appointment in the Physiology Department of the University in Edinburgh, where he also lectured in the Veterinary College. Later, in 1876, he was appointed Professor of Physiology at Glasgow University and then, in 1881, to be Fullerian Professor at the Royal Institution in London, an appointment which could be held along with his Glasgow appointment. McKendrick's early connection with Aberdeen, where he had of course been born, led to his building a house in Stonehaven to which he retired. He was made Provost of Stonehaven, and both he and his wife are buried in the churchyard of the ruined church of St Mary of the Storms perched on the clifftop north of the town.

When one looks at the ancient headstone erected to James McKendrick and Margaret Faichney in Ardoch Kirkyard it gives no clue to the fact that James McKendrick's grandson, educated at Braco School, was to achieve the highest academic honours and become internationally renowned. How many similar tales might be told of the other stones, often so corroded as to be completely indecipherable?

The Suicides' Graves

Before leaving the subject of graveyards, it is worth remembering that, in the past, those who committed suicide were not allowed to be buried in consecrated ground. It is possible that some suicides were buried near the chapel which existed in medieval times within the Roman Fort, but there is also an area in the middle of a forestry plantation near to the northern boundary of the parish, and lying between the Comrie road and the military road, which is marked on the Ordnance Survey map as 'Suicides' Graves'. This was presumably where at one time those who had taken their own lives were interred, but some were also buried behind the parish church on the side furthest away from the normal burial ground. Those who were buried here did apparently in some cases have gravestones erected, but of these only one still remains, set into the boundary wall.

The Toll Houses

Road maintenance in former times was financed by tolls which had to be paid by the users of the roads. There was a scale of charges, so much per head of cattle or sheep, rather more for a horse and cart, and so on. At one time there were four toll houses in the district. One was situated at the junction of the Feddal Road with the Crieff road, and, as we have seen, after being used as a Reading Room, it was ultimately demolished in the interests of road safety. The same fate befell another toll house at Balhaldie, while a third one, situated at Greenloaning opposite the Sheriffmuir road was occupied as a dwelling house until very recently when it too fell victim to the road makers when that stretch of the A9 was converted to dual carriageway.

The fourth toll house, on the north side of the Comrie road not far from its junction with the Crieff road, still exists as The Old Tollhouse and functions as a tearoom and therapy centre. Over a hundred years ago, in 1879, it was the roadman's house and was the scene of a murder. The roadman was an old man who lived alone, but who was regularly visited each morning by a young man who worked at the Mill of Ardoch on the River Knaik. Not getting an answer one morning to his knock, he informed the police who broke in and found the old man had been savagely beaten to death. A tramp was arrested and charged with his murder. Though the evidence was purely circumstantial, he was found guilty and hanged in Perth prison. There were those who felt that had the accused not been a vagrant, the court might have been less hasty in reaching a guilty verdict.

The Rottearns Toll House at Greenloaning, photographed around 1910.

Front Street in 1899 showing the Toll House at the corner of Feddal Road and the Ardoch Hotel on the left.

Some Agricultural Matters

Being mainly an agricultural parish, the majority of people were, in past times, employed in one way or another in the farming industry. Over the years this has changed with the changes in farming practice. Tractors have replaced the splendid pairs of Clydesdales which were a regular feature of the landscape, pulling plough or binder. The combine harvester has done away with the binding of corn into sheaves, setting them up in stooks to allow the sun and wind to complete the ripening and drying of the grain, carting the sheaves into the stackyard and later threshing the corn when the farm was visited by the itinerant threshing mill which had, in its turn, replaced the old horse mills the circular stone buildings for which can still be seen on many farms. All the old methods involved the employment of many men, and indeed gave occasional employment to their wives who would help with such tasks as stooking, thinning turnips and potato lifting. The hiring of farm workers took place at the Feeing Fairs which were held in Stirling, farmers and those seeking employment congregating at the top of King Street which became jammed with people. When a bargain was struck the farmer would give his prospective employee half-a-crown which made the bargain binding. On Fair days the public house at the top of the Arcade did a roaring trade!

At one time local farmers enjoyed an extra source of horses in the winter months. Four-in-hand carriages used to ply in the summer months transporting people from Aberfoyle to Inversnaid and from October to May the horses were given free to local farmers who had the use of them with only the cost of their feed to be met.

Not surprisingly, in a thriving agricultural community shows and competitions flourished. In the nineteenth century it is recorded that four fairs were held in Braco each year on the first Wednesday of January, the last Tuesday of April, the first Tuesday of August, and the last Tuesday of October. In addition, after the advent of the railway, cattle sales were held at Greenloaning in May and October, the cattle being conveniently transported to and from the sales by train. Ploughing matches were also a feature of the agricultural scene, and it was reported that on 10 March 1852:

> a grand ploughing match, open to all Scotland, was held on the farm of Greenloaning, possessed by Mr McEwen, and taken for cropping by Mr Anderson, Greenloaning Inn. The weather being very propitious, and the field being in the vicinity of the Greenloaning Station of the Scottish Central Railway, a numerous concourse of visitors was attracted. 29 Ploughs were early on the field, each directed by a stalwart ploughman. The judges were Messrs. Gardner, Rottearns; Finlayson, Pendreich; and Muirhead, Denny, and they had considerable difficulty in deciding the prizes offered by Mr McEwen, Blackdub owing to the excellence of the work.

However the judges finally awarded the prizes as follows: 1st William Muirhead, Pirnhall, Stirling; 2nd P. Lawrence, coal merchant, Greenloaning; 3rd Matthew Lennox Jr, Cullings, Ardoch.

The earliest agricultural society in the district was that of Dunblane which was founded on 1 January 1804 with the title of the Strathallan Farmers Club. As the name indicates, the Society was at first more intimately connected with the neighbourhood of Greenloaning which was then part of Dunblane Parish and the first president was an Ardoch man named William Anderson while the first treasurer was Harry Monteath of Greenloaning. Among the principal members were the tenants of Feddal, Cambushinnie and Balhaldie. The existence of this Strathallan Farmers Club as early as 1804 is perhaps responsible for the belief that the Ardoch Agricultural Society which today holds the Braco Show annually in July is the oldest society in the country. It appears that the Dunblane Show can probably trace its origins to the Strathallan Farmers Club, but nevertheless the Ardoch Agricultural Society can claim to be one of the oldest. There are records of its existence in 1843 and many believe that it was established before that. In its early days the Annual Show was mainly for cattle and was held in a field on the west side of the Crieff road before the junction with the Comrie road. Later it moved to where the Gentlecroft houses now are, then to the field behind the Village Hall, before finally being located in the Lodge Park. The Braco Show is today an important event which has grown considerably from its early days. While there is no longer a poultry section, nor indeed one for home-made butter, the entries, many of which come from a considerable distance, include cattle, sheep, goats, heavy horses, mules, ponies, and dogs. In recent years the Braco Show has been chosen as the venue for the Scottish Donkey Show with a large number of entries. In 1843 the Show was followed by a dinner and this was later replaced by a lunch, something which could

The War Memorial in 1922.

The War Memorial, 1999, showing the houses of Gentlecroft.

hardly be fitted into the present-day programme which now concludes with a dance which used to be held alternately at Netherton and Beannie Farms, but now takes place at the showground.

For a few years sheep dog trials were held in conjunction with the Show and these were among the first to be held in Scotland. The course was laid out in the Ardoch Estate across the Knaik from Gentlecroft. These trials were discontinued, but the same field was used in 1998 for the Scottish National Sheep Dog Trials.

The Second World War had a major effect on farming in this country. Land which had not previously been under the plough was brought into cultivation in order to maximise the country's production of grain, while subsidies were also given to encourage more acreage being given over to growing potatoes. While many were called up to serve in the forces, the importance of farming to the national war effort was recognised, and key workers were regarded as being in a reserved occupation and were exempt from conscription.

The parish also played host to service personnel. As has been mentioned, members of the Women's Land Army – the Land Girls – were billeted in Ardoch House, while members of the Cheshire Regiment and some Canadian units were encamped in the grounds of Ardoch Estate. After the evacuation from Dunkirk in 1940 the remnants of the Tank Corps arrived in the area, While some of the troops were camped in the grounds of Braco Castle, the tanks and their crews were unloaded at the sidings beside Carsebreck Loch which had been constructed in connection with the curling Bonspiels on the loch before the war. This was the last time that these sidings were used, and the Tank Corps commandeered the steading at Netherton Farm, where they remained until the following October when they moved to the Maltings in Blackford village. The tanks used to practise manoeuvres on Sheriffmuir, while guns sited near Cromlix used to fire across the valley to Sheriffmuir. The only bombs to fall in the parish during the war landed near Harperstone Farm, but whether the German plane responsible thought it was attacking something of military importance or, as is more likely, was merely ditching its load prior to returning to Germany is not known.

The War Memorial

Like most places in the country, men and women of Ardoch Parish made the ultimate sacrifice in both World Wars, and the new War Memorial in the village carries the names of twenty-two who fell in the First World War and an additional nine who gave their lives in World War II. The Memorial itself, a granite Iona Cross, was paid for by local collections after the First World War and erected opposite the foot of Smiddy Brae on land given by the Drummond Morays of Ardoch. An Armistice Day service is held at the Memorial each year by the Braco and Greenloaning branch of the Royal British Legion who renovated the ground round the Memorial, while Perth and Kinross Council provide fine floral displays in the surrounding flowerbeds.

Front Street and the War Memorial in 1922.

Front Street from the north, 1999.

Church Street, described as West End Terrace, in 1891 showing the Free Church and, in the distance, the Bog Green.

Church Street in the early years of the twentieth century with a 1910 Sunbeam 20 h.p. landolette, claret in colour, owned by Menzies Brothers of Henderson Street, Bridge of Allan, and probably in service as a taxi, at Glenorchy houses.

Braco in 1898 showing the Post Office with William Bayne at the door while at the foot of Cow Lane the two ladies in white aprons are perhaps from Aikman's Dairy. The Toll House jutting out at the corner of Feddal Road is clearly seen.

Braco, 1999, showing the Post Office and Dairy now converted into a private house.

Police, Medical and Veterinary Services

From the latter half of the nineteenth century Braco had a resident policeman who at one time lived in Church Street and who kept an eye on things in the village, moving on the tinkers camped on the Bog Green – where the Village Hall now is – when he felt they had been there long enough, or cuffing the ears of any youngster guilty of some misdemeanour, an action which, however effective, would not be permitted today. When the houses in Gentlecroft were built, one with suitable accommodation was allocated to the village policeman, but later this house came into private ownership when it was decided that Braco, after having had one for half a century, no longer required a resident policeman, its needs being adequately met from the police stations in Auchterarder and Crieff, and by visits from police patrol cars. Not everyone accepts this view, and many feel that a resident policeman on the beat would be to the benefit of the village. From time to time police officers do monitor the speed of traffic through the 30 miles per hour zone in the village resulting in some convictions for speeding, but in general the speed of cars, vans, and lorries in the village continues to be a problem. It is perhaps ironic to recall that in the 1920s a sign at either end of the village indicated that the maximum permissible speed in the village was 10 miles per hour!

There has never been a resident medical practitioner in either Braco or Greenloaning, the needs of the inhabitants being served at various times from Muthill, Blackford, Auchterarder, and Dunblane. Before the days of the motor car doctors used to travel by bicycle or on foot to visit their patients and many a long walk in bad weather they must have had. However, the advent of the car and of a motorised ambulance service, not to mention improved roads which were kept open in bad weather conditions, changed the situation. Today medical services for the parish are provided by the practices in Crieff and Dunblane. In both towns a well-equipped Health Centre exists where patients able to travel can be seen by appointment. Until recently both practices conducted surgeries in the village, although the problem of finding suitable accommodation has been a perpetual one. The use of a room in the Braco Hotel, though not without its problems, was acceptable to most but, with the change of ownership of the Hotel in 1998, this accommodation was no longer available. Arrangements were made to use the Church Hall and Vestry, and while the Crieff practice have continued to provide a surgery there once a week, the Dunblane practice have turned it down, though both groups have made it clear that house visits will be made if required. Full hospital facilities are available at Stirling and Perth Royal Infirmaries and the small hospital at Crieff has limited facilities including an Accident and Emergency Department.

The services of a District Nurse to supplement those provided by the General Practitioners became available after the end of the First World War. Funds were raised locally by door-to-door collections and other means to finance the appointment of a qualified nurse who was provided with accommodation in the Ardoch Inn. Further fund-raising efforts including garden fetes at Braco and Feddal Castles raised enough money to build a

Mike Boxer, present day Postmaster.

An envelope sent from Braco in 1850 bearing no postage stamp but with 'paid' handwritten and a circular 'paid' handstamp.

[*Those 'of rank or influence' were at one time entitle to free postal service, and this may be an example of such, although the sender is unknown. Rowland Hill vehemently opposed the practice of 'free' letters but perhaps it persisted in a small village like Braco. The envelope also carries a rectangular box stamp for Braco, typical of those used by many of the small village post offices which opened in the 1840s and 1850s.*]

house in Feddal Road for the District Nurse, and in 1946 this house and responsibility for the provision of district nursing services was taken over from the local Nursing Association by Perth and Kinross County Council. Nurse Kate Morris who retired in 1998 has not been replaced, and currently, just as in the case of the police, reliance has been placed on services from Auchterarder and Crieff.

In an agricultural community the ability to call on veterinary services is important, and the records show that John Thomson the veterinary surgeon in Braco in 1889 was succeeded in 1893 by Donald Wooley who remained for some forty years. Present-day veterinary service is available from, among others, the practices of Ashworth and Taylor in Crieff, Struthers and Scott in Doune, and Broadleys Veterinary Hospital in Stirling which is modern and well-equipped and which operates a branch surgery in Dunblane.

Shops and Trades

Today in Braco there are only two shops, a post office which also sells stationery, confectionery, greeting cards, and sundry other items, plus a grocer and newsagent, three motor repairers, together with a kitchen and bathroom designer, while Greenloaning has no shops at all. It is therefore difficult to imagine the situation not so many years ago when the range of trades and retail services available locally was vastly greater, and when, as one former resident of the village said, 'It didn't matter whether you wanted a suit or a pair of boots, you could have them made in the village.' There is little doubt that the greater mobility of the populace as a result of improvements in public transport and particularly the almost universal ownership of a motor car has led people to take their custom to the larger stores in neighbouring towns such as Stirling and Crieff or even Perth, with a greater choice on offer, rather than continue to patronise village traders and craftsmen.

A perusal of Leslie's *Directory of Perth and Perthshire* for a hundred years ago informs us that William Bayne was not only postmaster at Braco but also the bootmaker. Letters from all parts, collected from the train at Greenloaning, arrived at 7 a.m. and from Crieff at 10.30 p.m. Despatches to the north were made at 5 a.m., to all parts at 2 p.m. and 6.40 p.m., and to Crieff and the south at 10 p.m. It is interesting that even in these days of stricter Sabbath observance the post office was open on Sunday mornings at 9 a.m. to allow anyone to collect mail addressed to them which would otherwise not be delivered until the Monday morning. The ringing of the church bells, which were rung from 10 until 10.15 a.m. was the signal for the post office to close. At various periods in its history the post office has been located at the north end of Front Street and at the south end, where it is today.

Other traders and craftsmen listed for Braco are: William McKinnon, baker; Donald Wooley, blacksmith (was this the father of the vet?); John Henderson, coal merchant; Thomas Bayne, James Forbes & Co., Margaret McDiarmid, William McKinnon, Malcolm McRorie, and Janet White, all

The former mill at Greenloaning.

The sawmill on the Knaik as it was in 1950.

The cornmill on the Knaik in the 1890s.

grocers and general dealers; William Monteith, joiner; Malcolm McRorie, mason and builder; Isabella Miller, miller at Mill of Ardoch; and James Gilmour, tailor. For Greenloaning we have George Thomson, blacksmith; James Anderson and Alexander Ritchie, coal merchants; Thomas Stewart, joiner; and Andrew Edmonston, miller. There appeared to be no shops as such at Greenloaning though later there was a shop known as 'Jean's' which was situated opposite Mary Ann's Greenloaning Inn. Of course many of the shops in Braco had delivery vans, horse-drawn vehicles initially but motor vans later, and these served the needs of those who lived outwith Braco itself. Many of these businesses continued into the 1920s and 1930s and even after the end of the Second World War. Indeed the account of the parish in the *Third Statistical Account*, written in 1962 states:

> Braco is adequately supplied with shops, a Co-operative store, a baker's and grocer's shop, which caters by van for the farms, a sweet shop, two electricians' shops, and two cafes.

For many years Aikman's dairy existed in the lane which runs between Front Street and Mid Lane, hence the name Cow Lane. The byre was beside the dairy and the cows were grazed in the Roman camp, being walked from there to the dairy for milking. The dung from the byre was piled up beside the dairy and was removed by cart once a year. No one seems to have suffered any ill effects, but one wonders what present-day environmental health officers would have said about the arrangement!

With farming being the principal industry in the parish, it is not surprising to discover that there were several blacksmith's shops or smiddies where not only were shoes made and fitted to the horses which worked on the farms, but parts for ploughs, harrows and other equipment were manufactured or repaired. At one time there were as many as five smiddies in the area. One was situated beside the old toll house near the junction of the Crieff road with Feddal Road, while another was at the top of Smiddy Brae, and Braco Castle estate had its own smiddy. Outwith Braco village there was one at Greenloaning and another on the back road to Auchterarder at Seathaugh. None of these smiddies still exists.

Sawmills were also a feature. One was situated in Mid Lane opposite the end of Cow Lane, while another was on Braco Castle estate where the road to Blairmore leaves the steading road. This sawmill was powered by water, and though it is now ruinous, the roof having fallen in recent years, the remains of the waterwheel can still be seen. Another sawmill used to be at the west end of Carseview and beside it was a large shed where William Monteith the joiner carried out his business. This shed was sold to Mrs Graham of Braco Hotel and latterly it was used for keeping hens. At Greenloaning there was also a joinery business carried out by William McFarlane, while about 1941 the Forestry Commission established a sawmill at Greenloaning Station.

As has been said, there were, in the past, many shops and businesses in Braco. In Front Street, in the second house to the south of Cow Lane, at one time J.W. Monteith had a draper's shop at the front while a room at the

Front Street in 1898.

Front Street in 1950 showing the Gentlecroft houses still under construction.

Front Street, 1999.

Braco from the south around 1910. The Free Church steeple is obvious and the shed which can be seen at the west end of Carseview was where Monteith's joinery business was conducted.

back was, on certain days, used as a bank by the Bank of Scotland. The drapery was later taken over by David McIntosh who also carried out shoemaking, and still later the house became the village post office which moved from its earlier location at the other end of the village, a location to which it has now returned. Further down the street was the grocer and ironmonger, James Forbes & Co., whose premises were later taken over by the Co-operative Society. When it was no longer a grocery, and after a short period in the ownership of Etcetera, an upholstery and soft furnishing firm, it became a store for Kenneth Anderson Designs Limited. Behind Forbes the grocer, a shoemaking business was carried on in a wooden hut by George Hardie, while at the corner of Smiddy Brae was McKinnon's bakery. On the other side of Smiddy Brae, beyond the Braco Hotel, there was Reid's cycle repair shop and hairdresser run by the chauffeur from Braco Castle and his sons. Mr Reid senior provided hairdressing services in the evening. The Reids later established a garage and car-hiring business at the south end of the village where Sweeney's Garage is now. Beyond Reid's cycle repair shop were the premises of George Leggat the baker and grocer, who found himself in court in 1936 for having made one of his van drivers, James Cunningham, work longer than the permitted number of hours.

There were of course many other shops and businesses some of which lasted for only a short time. For a short period Mrs Janet Thomson sold sweets from one of the houses in Feddal Road opposite the Free Church. Beside the old Ardoch Inn a Miss Brown had a wool shop and dressmaking business, while the inn itself became a tearoom and ice cream shop. The Wee Cafe was run by James Anderson, who died in 1914, and whose son, also James Anderson, operated in 1926 the first bus service in the village. The Pioneer Bus, as it was called, ran from Crieff to Stirling by the Kinbuck road, and was later taken over by the General Omnibus Company. Another, cafe was the Red Rose Tearoom managed by John and Betty McArthur who subsequently took over the running of the village post office. The tearoom was situated beside the present Braco Shop of Margaret and David Adams. At one time A.M. Lauder supplied flowers, fruit and vegetables from the gardens at Ardoch House, but there never seems to have been either a butcher or a fishmonger in either Braco or Greenloaning, the needs of the inhabitants being presumably met by visiting vans.

Until recently Braco had a thriving potato industry run by the Rowe family. There were large storage sheds in Mid Lane immediately south of Smiddy Brae and many in the village found employment there grading and packing potatoes. The firm went out of business in the early 1990s and the sheds were demolished, the ground being designated for housing. Along Feddal Road a new industry has sprung up, much of the land formally used for agricultural purposes being devoted to the growing of Christmas Trees.

Local Government

Control of the civil affairs of the parish used to be in the hands of an elected Parish Council, but this was done away with in 1929, the County Council assuming overall responsibility for local government in the county, though some minor, though nevertheless important, issues were delegated to the District Council for West Perthshire. When Scottish local government was completely reorganised as a result of the 1973 Act, provision was made for the setting up of Community Councils which, while having no statutory duties or powers, were meant to act as a voice for the local community representing the views of the community to the local authority and other bodies operating in the area. The constitution of each community council was determined by the local authority and the Perth and Kinross District Council published its scheme on 1 January 1977 as a result of which the Braco and Greenloaning Community Council was set up with 6 elected members and a constitution which requires it to 'take such action as appears in the interests of the community to be expedient and practical'. The first meeting was held on 24 March 1977 when Mr James Dawson was elected chairman. Since then the Council has continued to meet regularly in either the Village Hall or the Church Hall in Braco and, for some of the meetings each year, in Greenloaning School.

Recreational and Social Activities

Mention has already been made of the attempts to provide the facilities of a reading room in the village, attempts which were ultimately abandoned, the books being dispersed, some to Innerpeffray Library. However, many other organisations have been formed over the years to provide for the social and recreational needs of those living in the area. Many of these are still thriving.

Perhaps one of the oldest is the Curling Club, though no one is quite sure when it was founded. A sketch in the Club's papers by a former vice-president, J. McKendrick Thomson, indicates that the Club was founded in 1750, but this may be artistic licence or wishful thinking. Certainly the Ardoch Curling Club was first affiliated to the Royal Caledonian Curling Club in 1845, but there is evidence that it was established much earlier. Among the presentation medals there is one dated 1844, and it is stated that the Royal Caledonian Curling Club has in its possession a curling stone dated 1700 which was presented to it by G.K. McCallum of Braco Castle. Was this stone discovered when the Castle gardens were being laid out, or did it indicate the existence of a very early club? We shall never know, and the only date which is definite is the date of affiliation, 1845. The Club expected to qualify for a Centenary Medal from the R.C.C.C. in 1945 but were disappointed to be told that there was a gap in the payment of their membership dues from 1913 until 1920 when payment was resumed.

In an attempt to have the R.C.C.C. have a change of heart, appealing letters were sent by the Ardoch Club secretary, Daniel Eadie, who wrote in one letter in January 1939, 'A few members are aware that some irregularity took place when the Club was in the hands of a very lax secretary and the majority of the enthusiastic members were answering their country's call'. But all appeals based on the exigencies of a wartime situation were in vain, and the Centenary Medal is not now due until 2020, a hundred years after the Club renewed its affiliation.

Curling was originally carried out on the ponds in Ardoch and Braco Castle estates when winter frost produced an adequate thickness of ice. Later, thanks to the generosity of Mr J. Finlay Muir of Braco Castle an asphalt rink was laid behind the Village Hall. This could be covered with a shallow layer of water which would freeze more quickly than the water in a pond. Electric lighting was provided by the generator in the Hall. There seem to have been problems with the surface of this rink which was finally abandoned, and the area has now been converted into tennis courts. In 1930 Major Falconer Stewart of Feddal Castle presented the Club with the Feddal Broom for competition between clubs within a ten mile radius of Braco. The names of the winners were engraved on the silver ring and the Broom was kept at Feddal Castle, each winner being presented with a miniature replica. The Club today curls indoors at the Perth Ice Rink.

The Royal Caledonian Curling Club itself organised great curling matches or Bonspiels on Carsebreck Loch at which clubs from all over competed whenever the ice was deemed thick enough to support the weight of all the people with their hampers of food and drink who were expected to attend. The competition was between clubs from the north and south sides of the Forth. The first Bonspiel was held in 1852 when it was reported that nearly six thousand people attended. Since then the event has taken place from time to time, but less frequently in the early part of the twentieth century as winters appeared to provide fewer adequately lengthy spells of hard frost. Sometimes, as in 1928, preparations reached the stage of the actual arrival of the competing curlers when the thaw would also arrive, rendering play impossible. A successful Bonspiel was held in 1929, and again in 1935 but

Braco Bowling Green and Gardens in the early 1900s showing the original wooden pavilion. The gardens are behind the Glenorchy houses, the Free Church cemetery can be seen on the right, while the ground across the road has now been built on.

Braco Bowling Green and Clubhouse with some members having a game, 1999.

this was the last one at Carsebreck. After the end of the Second World War the R.C.C.C. decided to move future Bonspiels to the Lake of Menteith but, at the time of writing, only one Bonspiel has taken place there.

A thriving and long-established recreational activity is bowling. Reference has been made earlier to the gift of land for a bowling green by Sir Renny Watson to commemorate the Diamond Jubilee of Queen Victoria in 1897. In the early days of the Braco Bowling Club many local residents were involved and often three generations of a family were all playing members. The original wooden pavilion has long since gone, and the Club house which replaced it has recently been refurbished providing a members' bar and new kitchen and toilet facilities. The outdoor bowling season runs from April to September during which social events are held to which non-members are welcomed. Throughout the winter months there are Club nights, whist drives and games evenings.

As a member of the West Perthshire Bowling Association and the Perthshire Bowling Association the Club has had many achievements in a variety of competitions. It also possesses a large number of cups and trophies given by local members which are competed for each year, and the Crawford Cup given by the Rev. Thomas Crawford of the Old House of Orchil for competition between the Club and Muthill Bowling Club.

Another organisation whose roots go back to the end of the nineteenth century is the Greenloaning Burns Club which, as has already been mentioned, was formed in 1889 in Mary Ann's Inn at Greenloaning, two of those who played an important part in its foundation being Andrew Edmonston the miller and Thomas Stewart the joiner who was the first secretary. The belief that Burns himself visited Mary Ann's has already been alluded to, and it is also said that there used to be a chair in Mary Ann's on which the poet had sat and on the arm of which he had scratched an

Braco Bowling Club members in the early 1900s.

inscription. Be that as it may, the Club, which is No. 116 on the roll of Burns Clubs, continues to thrive though it has had to move from Mary Ann's, which closed in the 1970s, first to the Allanbank, then to the Braco Hotel and now holds its annual Burns Supper on the first Friday of February in the Braco Village Hall. Members were drawn almost equally from Dunblane, Blackford, and Braco and Greenloaning. For several years in the mid-twentieth century the President was Daniel J. McIldowie who became President of the World Burns Federation, and in this capacity he visited Burns Clubs all over the world. On his return home he was presented with a medallion by the local Club.

Also in the late nineteenth century a Quoiting Club was formed which used to play behind where the Village Hall presently stands, but this sport has long been in abeyance in the area.

The Braco and Greenloaning Scottish Women's Rural Institute has a long history. It was founded in April 1918 by Mrs Muir of Braco Castle who, it is related, used to bring the women to the meetings in a farm cart. Originally it was in the Perth Federation, but owing to the difficulty and inconvenience of travelling to Perth, members were unable to enter fully into the activities of the Perth Federation and in 1952 it transferred to the Stirling and West Perthshire Federation. Apart from the regular monthly meetings from September to April, there are coffee mornings, whist drives, a theatre outing, an annual dinner, and a Christmas party.

The Allanwater Young Farmers Club was established in 1948 by Daniel J. McIldowie and Abe Broadfoot and the first meeting was held at Nether Cambushinnie on the last Saturday of July in that year, John McColl of Loig being elected the first chairman. The Club covers the areas of Braco, Greenloaning, and Blackford, and although its present membership is small it enjoys some success at both district and national young farmers events. Meetings may consist of a talk by an invited speaker or a visit to a place of interest. There is a strong emphasis on fund raising with the Club giving a donation to charity each year. Every Christmas a bag of vegetables, firewood, or shortbread is distributed to the pensioners in Braco.

The Ardoch Amateur Dramatic Society was formally constituted in 1975 but for some twelve years before that a group of people in the village who were interested in amateur dramatics had put on concerts and plays, produced by Jean Rowe, and under the banner of the Allanwater Young Farmers or the Church, to raise funds for, for example, new carpets and new heating in the Church. In the late 1960s the summer outing for the pensioners of Braco and Greenloaning became the objective and this tradition still remains today.

Following on the drawing up of a constitution in 1975 the Society moved away from the concert party image and offered full-length plays and under the chairmanship of Margaret Gray productions of a very high standard were presented. The Society has always been fortunate in having a number of members who could give their expertise in developing the technical side of the productions, and help with lighting systems, curtains, scenery, and costumes have all helped to add a professional touch. Occasional productions have taken place outwith Braco. For example, two plays were presented in Dunblane in aid of Strathcarron Hospice, and support was also given to the provision of new seating in the Studio Theatre in the MacRobert Arts Centre in Stirling University by performances during the fund raising period and at the gala opening of the refurbished theatre. Every second year a pantomime is produced involving a large cast of adults and children and incidentally giving many of the children in the village their first taste of live theatre. This is always a very enjoyable occasion, but the number involved on the stage and behind the scenes is so large that a pantomime every year is not possible. In 1982 the construction of a demountable apron stage gave an added dimension to the hall stage, allowing action to be continuous while scene changes took place behind the curtain – an essential ingredient for pantomime. The part of the 'dame' in the biannual pantomime is generally played magnificently by Jim Dawson who has been involved with the Society's productions since the early days in the 1960s and, in recognition of his stalwart service, he was, in 1988, made the first Honorary President. The present postmaster, Mike Boxer, has been closely involved with the productions since 1980 and the post office currently functions as the box office for productions.

The Braco and Greenloaning branch of the Royal British Legion Scotland is another organisation, open to all ex-service men and women, which also supports the pensioners of the parish, providing a pre-Christmas lunch in the Allanbank Hotel. Funds for this event are raised at a ceilidh and dance held usually in October. The Branch was responsible for having the garden round the War Memorial renovated and, in addition to providing a social focus for its members, also helps organisations in the district in many ways.

Horse riding is available at the Equestrian Centre which is situated across the A9 on the Sheriffmuir Road.

Badminton and tennis are also available in the village. There are two badminton groups which play in the Village Hall, one in the afternoon and the other in the evening. The Tennis and Sports Club is fairly recent, having been set up in 1997. The tennis courts behind the Hall have been brought up to standard and an enthusiastic group have organised a mixed doubles tournament and also a singles championship.

After the First World War a football team, known as Braco Football Team, was established and played in the Crieff and District Juvenile League which included teams from a large number of places in south and west Perthshire. Matches were played on a pitch in the Boghead Park behind where the Braco Hall now stands. Later, in 1937, a second team with the name of Braco Thistle was formed, and this also took part in league matches. Greenloaning had a five-a-side team which was involved in the matches which featured regularly after the cattle shows. After the end of the Second World War the League was not revived, and today the only football played are occasional matches organised by the Allanwater Young Farmers.

Several organisations are run, or have been started, under the wing of the Church. The Women's Guild meets once a month, with a varied programme of speakers, but the Boys' Brigade, the Life Boys, and the Girls' Guildry, which once existed, do so no longer. The Ardoch Scottish Country Dancing Club was formed in 1971 by Miss Chris Duff and met in the school.

New Muir Homes housing estate under construction at Greenloaning, 1999.

In 1973 it was taken over by Ian Kinroy who continued to teach dances old and new until 1988, the venue changing first to the Bowling Club pavilion and then to the Church Hall. Since 1988 Charles Robertson has taken over the leadership and the Club continues to be a popular recreation. More recently the Ardoch Church Gardening Club has been formed and meets every second month, when talks are given which appeal not only to the keen gardener but also to the beginner. Flower arranging classes are held and each summer the Club members produce a beautiful garden of flowers in the Church grounds.

The needs of the younger members of the community are met in a number of ways. There is a Mothers and Toddlers group which meets regularly during the school terms and caters for children from birth to the age of 3. Then there is the Braco 3–5 Playgroup and a nursery for pre-school children has recently been set up at Whistlebrae. In the early 1970s a Youth Club was started by the headmaster of Braco School, Mr Ian Kinroy, and the minister of Ardoch Church, the Rev. Dugald McKinnon. It met in the Village Hall and badminton and table tennis were among the activities. Later Willie Bayne and Jim Dawson took over the Club and ran it for some fifteen years, when leadership fell to Glen Johnstone and Bob Jones with assistance for a short time from David Yorke. After another ten years enthusiasm waned somewhat, largely because no one could be found to take over the responsibility of leadership. Recently, however, plans have been made to revive the Club, and there are hopeful signs that it will flourish again under Chris Henry and Lorna Taylor.

Though the years have seen many changes in the parish, it is in good heart and can look forward to the twentyfirst century with confidence.

Index

Adair's map of Strathearn: 16
Adam, William: 35
Adams, David and Margaret: 70
Agricola: 12
Aikman's Dairy: 62, 67
al Tajir, Mohammed: 45
Albert, Prince: 17
Allan, River: 11, 12
Allanbank Hotel: 35, 38, 41, 74, 75
Allanwater Young Farmers Club: 74
Amateur Dramatic Society: 74
Anderson, James: 67, 69
Anderson, Mary Ann: 39
Anderson, William: 57
Antonine Wall, the: 12
Ardoch Agricultural Society: 57
Ardoch Church: 23, 26, 30
Ardoch Estate: 17, 20, 22, 43, 45, 51, 59
Ardoch House: 16, 17, 20, 43, 45, 46, 59, 70
Ardoch Inn: 22, 35, 63, 69
Ardoch Manse: 24, 26
Ardoch, Roman fort: 11
Ardochlea: 22, 35
Argyll, Duke of: 16, 45, 46
Auchterarder: 51, 63

Badminton: 75
Bakers: 65, 67, 69
Balhaldie: 55, 57
Bank of Scotland: 69
Bayne, Thomas: 65
Bayne, William: 62, 65, 76
Beannie Farm: 59
Big Well: 22
Bishop's Bridge: 18
Black Ford, the: 11
Blackford: 11, 15, 21, 26, 51, 59, 73, 76
Blacksmith's shops: 67
Blairinroar: 14
Blairmore: 67
Bog Green: 24, 34, 41, 61, 63
Boghead Park: 75
Bonspiels: 59, 71, 73
Bowling Club: 47, 52, 73

Boxer, Mike: 64, 75
Boys' Brigade: 75
Braco: 7, 14, 18, 21, 27, 42, 43, 47, 53, 54, 63
Braco Castle: 21, 47, 48, 59
Braco Estate: 46
Braco Free Church: 24, 26
Braco Hotel: 35–37, 63, 74
Braco School: 25, 34, 35
Braco Show: 57
Braco Thistle: 75
Bridgend: 22
Brig o' Ardoch: 22
British Legion: 59, 75
Broadfoot, Abe: 74
Brown, Miss: 69
Brown-Douglas, F.A.: 48
Brydie, Andrew: 53
Burns Club: 39, 73
Burns, Robert: 39
Bus Service: 69
Buttergask Farm: 21

Cafes: 67, 69, 70
Calder and Watson: 42
Camelon: 12, 13
Camps Castle: 13
Carsebreck Loch: 59, 71
Carseview: 67, 69
Caulfeild, Edward: 20
Chapel Hill: 17
Chapel of Ease: 23, 24, 27
Chapel Raith: 17
Christmas Trees: 70
Church Session House: 31, 34
Church Street: 27, 63
Clayton, General: 20
Clerk, Sir John: 16
Clock Tower: 25
Coal merchants: 57, 65, 67
Coates, Ken and Doris: 35
Community Council: 19, 70
Comrie: 12, 51
Conchie, J.: 48
Confectioners: 65
Coupans Farm: 23

Cow Lane: 62, 67
Crawford Cup: 52, 73
Crawford, Rev. Thomas: 52, 73
Crichton, Marion: 45
Crieff: 19, 35, 41, 63, 65
Crofthead Farm: 48
Cunningham, James: 69
Curling Club: 71
Cuthbert, James G.: 25, 27, 29
Cycle repairers: 69

Dairy: 62, 67
Dalginross: 12
Dalpatrick: 14
Dark Ages: 14
Dawson, J.: 70, 75, 76
Deaf Knowe: 11
District Nurse: 63
Drapers: 67
Dressmakers: 69
Drummond Castle: 15–17
Drummond, Lord: 15, 16
Drummond, Patrick: 19
Duff, Chris: 75
Dunblane: 12, 14, 35, 39, 57, 63, 65, 74, 75
Dunblane Cathedral: 15

Eadie, Daniel: 71
Eadie, James: 36
Eadie, Janet: 53
Edmonston, Andrew: 67, 73
Electricians: 67
Equestrian Centre: 75
Etcetera: 69

Faichney, Margaret: 53, 54
Fairs: 56, 57
Feddal Castle: 48, 71
Feddal Estate: 48
Feddal Road: 27, 41, 48, 53, 55, 65, 67, 69, 70
Feeing Fairs: 56
Flower Show: 39
Football: 75
Forbes, James & Co.: 65, 69
Free Church: 24–27, 34, 61, 69
Free Church School: 27

Front Street: 22, 37, 56, 60, 65, 67, 68

Garages: 37, 69
Gardening Club: 76
Garrick Cottage: 20
Gask, House of: 52
General Omnibus Company: 70
Gentlecroft: 37, 57, 59, 63, 68
George III: 46
Gilmour, James: 67
Girls' Guildry: 75
Gordon, Alexander: 16
Graemes of Orchil: 51, 52
Graham, James Gillespie: 52
Grahams of Braco Castle: 46
Gray, Margaret: 74
Green Well: 22
Greenloaning: 14, 18, 25, 26, 35, 41–43, 55, 57
Greenloaning Church: 26
Greenloaning Farm: 14, 35
Greenloaning Inn: 67
Greenloaning School: 35
Greenloaning Station: 41, 42, 65, 67
Grinnan Hill: 9, 14, 17
Grocers: 65, 67, 69
Gunnocks: 18

Hadrian's Wall: 12
Hairdressers: 69
Haldane of Gleneagles: 19
Halley, Jim: 41
Harperstone Farm: 59
Helen, Queen: 11
Henderson, John: 65
Henry, Chris: 76
Horse riding: 75
Hunterian Museum: 15

Inchmahome Priory: 17
Ironmongers: 69

Johnstone, Glen: 76
Joiners: 67, 69
Jones, Bob: 76

Kaims Castle: 13, 14
Keir Burn: 53

Keir Estate: 43
Kenneth Anderson Designs: 69
Kinbuck: 11
Kinroy, Ian: 76
Kitchen and Bathroom Designers: 65
Knaik, River: 12, 18–20, 22, 55, 59

Larbert: 12, 30, 41, 53
Lauder, A.M.: 70
Leggat, George: 69
Life Boys: 75
Lindum: 12
Lodge Park: 18, 57
Lollius Ubricus, Governor: 12

Machany Water: 11, 18
MacOwan, J.B.: 29
MacRobert Arts Centre: 75
Mar, Earl of: 45
Mary Ann's Inn: 35, 39, 67, 73, 74
Masons: 19, 67
Masterton, James: 21
McArthur, John and Betty: 70
McCallum, G.K.: 24, 47, 71
McColl, John: 74
McDiarmid, Margaret: 65
McFarlane, William: 67
McIldowie, Daniel J.: 7, 74
McIntosh, David: 69
McKendrick, James: 53, 54
McKendrick, John G.: 52
McKinnon, Rev. Dugald: 24, 76
McKinnon, William: 65
McLeod, Jim: 24
McRorie, Malcolm: 65, 67
Medical Services: 63
Mid Lane: 22, 67, 70
Mid lane: 39
Middle Feddal Farm: 48
Mill Hill Road: 39
Miller, Isabella: 67
Millers: 67, 73
Millhill Drive: 14
Monoliths: 11
Mons Graupius: 12
Monteath, Harry: 57
Monteith, J.W.: 67
Monteith, William: 67

Moray, Charles: 43
Morris, Nurse Kate: 65
Mothers and Toddlers group: 76
Motor Repairers: 65
Muir, Commander Robin: 48
Muir, J.F.: 39, 48, 71
Muir, Mrs: 30, 39, 48, 74
Muir, Nicholas: 48
Muir of Orchil: 13, 15
Murray, Lord George: 19
Muthill: 14, 15, 19, 22, 23, 27, 63

Ness, Patrick: 47
Netherton Farm: 21, 59
Newsagents: 65
Nisbet, Robin and Mandy: 39
Nursing Services: 65

Ochiltree, Bishop Michael: 18
Old House of Orchil: 14, 51, 52, 73
Orchil Barony: 51
Orchil House: 13, 50, 52
Oxford, Lord: 16

Pack Horse Bridge: 18
Pennant, Thomas: 16
Perth Music Festival: 31
Pioneer Bus: 69
Playgroup: 76
Ploughing Matches: 57
Pococke, Richard: 16
Police: 63
Polton Hall: 39
Post Office: 62, 64, 65, 69, 70, 75
Potato Holidays: 29
Praetorium: 16
Pugin, A.W.: 52
Pullar, E.: 48

Quarter Session minutes: 19
Queen Helen: 11
Quoigs Farm: 14
Quoiting Club: 74

Railway: 41
Raspberry Growing: 42
Reid's Cycle Repairers: 69
Reid's Garage: 69

Ritchie, Alexander: 67
Rob Roy: 49, 51
Robertson, Charles: 76
Rottearns: 42, 51, 55
Roundel Stone: 14
Roundel, The: 14
Rowe, Jean: 74
Rowe's Potatoes: 70
Roy, General William: 16
Royal Caledonian Curling Club: 71

Sawmills: 66, 67
School log: 25, 27, 29–31
Schools: 27
Scottish Country Dancing Club: 75
Severus, Emperor: 12
Sheriffmuir, Battle of: 16
Shoemakers: 69
Sibbald, Sir Robert: 16, 17
Silverton Farm: 48, 53
Smiddies: 67
Smiddy Brae: 22, 39, 59, 67, 69, 70
Smith Art Gallery and Museum: 7, 14
St Blane: 14
St Fillan: 14
St Patrick: 14
Standing Stones: 11
Stewart, Major J. Falconer: 48, 71
Stewart, Thomas: 67, 73
Stirling: 12, 56, 63, 65
Stirling, Henry: 45
Stirling, Major W.M.: 17
Stirling, Robert: 43
Stirling, Sir Henry: 16
Stirling, Sir James: 43
Stirling, William: 43
Stobie's Map: 9
Stone Circles: 11
Stonehaven: 54
Strageath: 13, 14
Straid: 14
Strathallan Farmers Club: 57
Strathallan Park: 14
Strathcarron Hospice: 75

Struthill: 14
Suicides' Graves: 54
Sweeney's Garage: 69

Tacitus: 12
Tailors: 67
Taylor, Lorna: 76
Tennis and Sports Club: 75
Thomas, Rev.: 16
Thomson, George: 67
Thomson, James McKendrick: 53, 71
Thomson, John: 53, 65
Thomson, Mrs Janet: 69
Thornton, G.B.: 48
Toll Houses: 21, 48, 55, 56, 62
Topfold Farm: 21
Tutor of Ardoch, The: 43

United Presbyterian Church: 25
University of Glasgow: 15, 16, 30, 54

van Ballegooljen, Mr and Mrs M.: 48
Veterinary Services: 63
Victoria, Queen: 17, 47
Village Hall: 24, 30, 31, 39, 48, 63, 70, 74–76

Wade, General: 20
War Memorial: 58, 59, 75
Waterside: 22
Watson, Sir William Renny: 47
Whistlebrae: 76
Whistlebrae Farm: 48
White, Janet: 65
White, John: 25
Women's Guild: 75
Women's Land Army: 45, 59
Women's Rural Institute: 74
Wooley, Donald: 65
World War I: 30, 48, 59
World War II: 20, 22, 34, 45, 59

Young Farmers Club: 74
Youth Club: 76